Women and Men in the Light of Eden

A practical commentary on the three "Eden passages"

Genesis 1-3
Ephesians 5-6
1 Timothy 1-3

with discussion questions

Bruce C. E. Fleming

XULON PRESS

*Women and Men
in the Light of Eden*
by Bruce C. E. Fleming

Printed in the United States of America

ISBN 9781615796908

This practical commentary is written in basic English for international use and for ease of translation into other languages.

www.xulonpress.com

TABLE OF CONTENTS

About the author

B ruce C. E. Fleming is the author of numerous articles and reports, including as Secretary for the "Authority and Uniqueness of Scripture Report" in the (ICOWE) *Lausanne Congress Compendium* (1975). He is author of *Contextualization of Theology: an Evangelical Assessment* (1980), the *Think Again Series on Women and Men, 1-8* (2003), and *Familiar 'Leadership' Heresies Uncovered* (2005).

He holds three graduate and post-graduate degrees from Trinity Evangelical Divinity School, Deerfield, Illinois, and from the University of Strasbourg, France.

Ordained by the Evangelical Free Church of America, he served as a church-planting pastor in the United States, Europe and Congo (DRC). He trained pastors from French-speaking countries in Africa as Professor of Practical Theology and Academic Dean of the Bangui Evangelical Graduate School of Theology (BEST/FATEB) in the Central African Republic.

He has widely traveled in the United States, Europe and Africa. He has consulted and written on training in practical theology for churches in Africa and beyond.

Acknowledgements

My wife, Joy, did the groundbreaking work on the Hebrew text of Genesis 3:16 in context (Genesis 2-3). Her doctoral research made clear what the Bible did, and did not say. I was able to think again about this and other Bible passages on women and men, thanks to her.

We have been married more than 30 years and have two adult children and one grandchild. We have been supported by the love and prayers of our family members, our church, and by our brothers and sisters in Christ who speak English, French, Lingala and other languages.

Soli Deo Gloria!

Minneapolis, 2011

"… that they may be encouraged in heart and united in love, so that they may have the full riches of complete understanding, in order that they may know the mystery of God, namely, Christ, in whom are hidden all the treasures of wisdom and knowledge." – Colossians 2:2-3 (NIV)

Chapter One

Together with God in the Garden

In the beginning (Genesis 1:1-2:3)

W ho wrote — "in the beginning" — after talking with God? Two people did! Moses did in Genesis 1:1 and John did in John 1:1. Each talked with God like a friend (Exodus 33:11, John 13:22-26).

Moses talked with God in the desert for forty years and wrote "in the beginning" using Hebrew words. John talked with Jesus for three years and wrote "in the beginning" using Greek words.

Is that clear? Your Bible is a translation into English from the Hebrew Old Testament and the Greek New Testament. Some languages are better at saying certain things than other languages. When Hebrew words and Greek words are translated, sometimes it is hard to translate the meaning clearly into the modern language. Sometimes it takes more than one word in English to translate a Hebrew or a Greek word from the Bible.

God speaks through the Bible. It doesn't change. But, modern languages change from year to year. Translations need to be updated from time to time. Our memories of what we have learned from the Bible need to be refreshed from time to time. It is good to think again about the Bible.

Who created? It was revealed to Moses and the people of Israel there was only "one" God, "Hear O Israel: The Lord our God, the Lord is one" (Deuteronomy 6:4). The Hebrew word used for "one" was *'echad*. It came from a root word meaning to unify or collect together. This Hebrew word was used in Genesis 2:24 for the two shall be "one" flesh.

In Genesis 1:1, the word used for "God" in Hebrew was *elohim*. Its ending with the two Hebrew letters "*-im*" was like ending an English word with the letter "*-s.*" There was only one Creator in the beginning. Could there be a better way to translate that Hebrew word for "God" to show that the word ended with "*-im*"?

What does it say? The Bible rolls out further details as one sentence follows a previous sentence, one passage follows a previous passage, and one book follows a previous book. Especially when the Bible is introduced to the people of a culture where it has not been taught before, it is important to get right the meaning of the first chapters of the Bible.

A careful look at the verses of the first chapter of Genesis shows that God Three-in-One was at work. The *Father* Three-in-One created "in the beginning" (Genesis 1:1) The *Spirit* was at work during creation (Genesis 1:2). The *Word* (Jesus Christ) was at work in creation too (Genesis 1:3, John 1:1-3). Therefore, God Three-in-One was involved in creation: the Father, the Spirit and the Word!

In many languages it is not possible to use a unified word like "God" or "one" every time it is needed. Yet, this is how it was written in Hebrew in Genesis 1:1: "God" (combined word) "created" (singular action word).

Many, if not most, translations have opted to use a single word for "God" and a single action word, too in the opening verses of Genesis. This way of translating has seemed to rule out the action of God in three persons "in the beginning."

Here is a possible way to communicate what happened on Day 1 of Creation (Genesis 1:1-3):

The Father Three-in-One created the heavens and the earth.
The Spirit Three-in-One hovered over the dark waters of the earth.
The Word Three-in-One said, "Let there be light," and there was light.

In Days 2, 3 and 4, the Word Three-in-One spoke more of creation into existence. The Father Three-in-One saw that it was "good."

On Day 5 of Creation, the creatures of the water and the birds of the sky were created. "It was good" (Genesis 1:21). Then they were blessed, "Be fruitful and increase in number and fill the water in the seas, and let the birds increase on the earth" (Genesis 1:22).

These were God's first words of blessing. They had to do with having offspring.

Day 6 — in three parts. During the first part of Day 6 of Creation, the Word Three-in-One spoke and created the land creatures, "'Let the land produce living creatures according to their kinds....' And it was so." (Genesis 1:24-25). "It was good."

During the second part of Day 6 of Creation, the first two humans were specially made, "Let us make humankind in our image, in our likeness ... male and female...." (Genesis 1:26-27).

Many details of their creation were described in Genesis 2:4-25. At the end of these detailed verses, God had united them in the special relationship of marriage, and the man and the woman were together with God in the Garden of Eden.

During the third part of Day 6 of Creation, God was with the man and the woman. Just as God blessed the birds and the fish at the end of Day 5, God blessed the man and woman at the end of Day 6. They were to have many offspring. Their children would fill the earth.

Then, God told them to rule over the other living beings on the earth. "Rule over the fish of the sea and the birds of the air and over every living creature that moves on the ground" (Genesis 1:28, Psalm 115:16). After all was accomplished by the end of Day 6, creation was "very good" (Genesis 1:31).

The details given in Genesis chapter 2:4-25 fitted into Genesis 1:-2:3 in this way:

First part of Day 6. Genesis 1:24-25
Second part of Day 6.
- Introduction: Genesis 1:26
- In brief: Genesis 1:27
- In detail: Genesis 2:4-24
Third part of Day 6. Genesis 1:28-31, 2:25.

***

In the Garden of Eden (Genesis 2:4-3:25)

Genesis 2:4-24 told how on Day 6 God put everything in place and began a wonderful relationship with the first two human beings. Their relationship in the Garden of Eden was summarized in Genesis 2:25.

In Genesis 3:1-5, sometime after Day 7, Satan attacked the woman and the man. He lied to them seeking to bring about their deaths. In response to Satan's words, they each took a bite of the forbidden fruit. Their life after death, and how God dealt with them and with Satan, was told in Genesis 3:7-24.

The first human with God (Genesis 2:7-17). On Day 6 of creation, God planted a Garden in Eden. God caused to grow every tree that was pleasing to the sight and every fruit tree that was good for food. In the Garden, there were two one-of-a-kind fruit trees: the tree of life, and the tree of the knowledge of good and evil. A river flowed in the Garden of Eden to water it.

Outside of the Garden, God made the first human being from the dust of the ground and breathed the breath of life into his nostrils. The adult human met God, his Creator, where he was taken from the dust.

The Hebrew word for "human" was "*adam.*" This word was not a name.

God took the man and put him into the Garden of Eden. God spoke to the man about the Garden. He was to cultivate it and keep it.

The Garden of Eden was different from the world outside of it. It was a place for work, beauty, food, and for walking with God. Did the man judge that God had made a good home for him inside the Garden?

The man was not lonely in the Garden. The man and God were together in the Garden of Eden. The Creator of all things built a loving relationship with the one human being. In this way, God demonstrated the worth of each and every individual human being.

All the fruit of the trees in the Garden was good to eat. But it was not God's will for the fruit from one of the trees to be eaten, the tree of the knowledge of good and evil. God commanded the man, "You are free to eat from any tree in the garden, but you must not eat from the tree of the knowledge of good and evil, for in the day you eat of it you will surely die" (Genesis 2:17).

The man heard God's words and understood God's will. He could freely eat from all the trees, except one. He learned from God the consequence of taking a bite from the tree of the knowledge of good and evil.

The man had a will and an example to follow. Everything God created was good. He could follow God's example and do good and he could obey God's commandment. He could freely eat from every tree in the Garden except one.

Two humans together with God (Genesis 2:18-25). In the middle of Day 6, God was not ready to bless just the one human to multiply and fill the Earth. The creation of humankind was not yet finished. God would bless two humans joined together, a man and a woman, to be fruitful and multiply.

God told the man about that final step in creation. God told the man that it was "not good" for him to be the only human being. God would make a woman. Then, God could bless the human race.

**On Day 6 it was not enough for the man
to be the only human being.**

Before creating the woman, God gave the man a task to do. God brought the beasts of the field and the birds of the air to the man to see what he would name them. The man saw the different kinds of livestock, birds and beasts. He decided what the name of each kind would be. The man saw that these other kinds of beings were not like him.

To describe the other human being God planned to make, two different Hebrew words were used (*'ezer* and *kenegdo*). The first word in English meant "strong-ally." The second meant "corresponding-to."

The Bible in other places used the same word "strong-ally" for God or for rulers (for example, Deuteronomy 33:7, Psalm 121:1-2, Isaiah 30:1-5). The man and the woman would be "strong allies." Like rulers, they would be "corresponding-to" one another.

To create the other human, God put the man in a deep sleep. God built the woman from a rib of the body of the man. The woman was made in God's image and likeness.

In the Garden, the woman first met God, her Creator. Each of them, the man and the woman, first knew God, their Creator, before they knew one another. Each one was made in the image and likeness of God.

After that, God brought them together. The man saw that she was a human like him. He saw that she was the female human (*ishah*), and that he was the male human (*ish*).

When God brought them together, it was the start of their marriage relationship. The woman, who was with God, was greeted by the man who rejoiced.

No other marriage was like this first one. They had no human parents or other family members when they were joined together by God.

***

The marriage model. The first man and woman were joined by God in the first marriage relationship. Their marriage was a model for every marriage!

In the beginning, each one knew God before they knew each other. Every man and woman should be in a right relationship with God *before marriage*. Each should be in a right relationship with God *during marriage*. Should the other spouse die first, the remaining one should continue in a right relationship with God *after marriage*.

The marriage relationship was good and pure. There was no sin in the first marriage relationship. In marriage, they were unashamed before God and one another. Both the man and the woman had two good and right relationships — with God and with their partner in marriage.

God joined them together for life. In the beginning, there was no death. And there was no plan for divorce (Matthew 19:8).

Taking the first marriage as their model, all other couples had four steps to take in marriage, according to Genesis 2:22-25.

1. In God's eyes (Genesis 2:22). God brought together in marriage the first two adults, the man and the woman. They began their marriage relationship in the presence of God.

2. The man left his parents (Genesis 2:24). The man left his father and mother. This was done on the beginning day of the new marriage relationship. It was a public step. When the man left them, his family and others knew it. The Bible did not say the woman left her family. The man did.

3. The husband committed himself to his wife (Genesis 2:24). The man's closest relationship was no longer with his father and mother but with his wife. After his relationship to God, a husband had no greater commitment in life than his commitment to his wife.

The Bible used the Hebrew action word, "to-commit" (*davaq*), only three times. The first was here in Genesis 2. The second was of Solomon to his love. The third was of daughter-in-law, Ruth, to Naomi.

Here is what it meant for Ruth "to-commit" to Naomi (Ruth chapter 1): *With you* I will go and lodge. *Your people* will be my people. *The true Lord* whom you worship is my Lord and God. *For all our days*, my commitment is to you.

4. They united (Genesis 2:24). The husband and wife became "one flesh." This union was both sexual and emotional.

No further steps were required in the Bible. Whether a couple had children, or had no child at all, changed nothing about the fact that their united relationship in marriage before God was complete. Like the first married couple in the Garden of Eden, they were strong allies, corresponding to one another, united by God for life.

***

In the third part of Day 6, God blessed the first man and woman to be fruitful and multiply and fill the earth with their children (Genesis 1:28a). This blessing was like the one God made at the end of Day 5 to the fish and to the birds.

God also gave them the responsibility to rule over every other kind of living being. "Rule over the fish of the sea and the birds of the air and over every living creature that moves on the ground" (Genesis 1:28b).

God did not tell one of them to rule over the other one. God was over all.

What would they and their children eat? What would they feed the living creatures they ruled over? God had planned for all this and told them:

I give you every seed-bearing plant on the face of the whole earth and every tree that has fruit with seed in it. They will be yours for food. And to all the beasts of the earth and all the birds of the air and all the creatures that move on the ground — everything that has the breath of life in it — I give every green plant for food. (Genesis 1:29-30)

At the end of Day 6, what was God's evaluation of all the work of Creation? "God saw all that he had made, and it was very good" (Genesis 1:31). How wonderful! The man and woman saw reasons for the judgment God made and could agree.

Every man and woman who hears what happened at creation learns that they too are in God's image! They learn that God's work of creation was very good (Romans 1:20).

The details of what took place during the Days of Creation were a revelation from God! What it was like "in the beginning" could only be told by one who was there before the man and the woman were created. We have the great privilege of learning this from God's Word, the Bible, in Genesis 1-2.

***

God had also created millions of blameless angels (Revelation 5:11). They were messenger spirits. They were not like the earthly beings. The angels praised God, served God, and obeyed God (Psalm 103:20). The most wonderful of these blameless spirits, Lucifer, had been in the Garden of Eden (Ezekiel 28:13).

But, Lucifer lifted up his heart in pride and corrupted his wisdom. He rebelled against God in order to rule over God!

Some of the other angels rebelled with Lucifer, who was also called Satan, and they became demonic spirits (Isaiah 14:13-14, Ezekiel 28:12-17, Revelation 12:9). How twisted!

***

Attack, defeat and God's response (Genesis 3:1-19)

Satan attacked the two (Genesis 3:1-4). Not long after Day 7 of Creation, a strange voice spoke to the woman and man in the Garden of Eden. This was when they were near the tree of life and the tree of the knowledge of good and evil.

It was not God's voice. It was not the man's voice. It was not the woman's voice. It was the voice of another. It came out of a serpent, a creature made by God.

Satan, the rebellious fallen angel, spoke through the body of that serpent. What about Satan's words through the serpent in the Garden of Eden? Jesus described Satan in these words: "from the beginning," Satan was "a murderer" and the "father of lies" (John 8:44).

Satan came to kill the two persons created in the image and likeness of God. Satan used lies to accomplish this. He lied to the woman. He lied to the man as well. He used the plural Hebrew word "you-two" which included both humans.

Satan's words were wildly incorrect — "Did God really say, 'You must not eat from any tree in the garden'?" He mocked God's good judgment by suggesting God had said not to eat from any of the wonderful trees!

On Day 6, God had given the man and the woman the authority to rule over serpents as well as all the other living creatures. The woman corrected the serpent's foolish words and instructed it. Only one tree was forbidden, on pain of death.

At this point, the strange voice flatly contradicted God. "You-two surely will not die!" Satan lied about the outcome of eating the fruit.

Then, the rebellious angel turned the focus from God's words to the fruit. God never intended for that fruit to be eaten. To eat would bring death! It would not be good in any way to disobey God and die.

Two Bites (Genesis 3:6-7). The "father of lies" deceived the woman. It was true that the trees in the garden gave good food. Perhaps this fruit would be good to eat if it opened one's eyes, as the serpent claimed.

The woman, after she was deceived, took some and ate it. She gave it to the man who was right there with her and he ate it.

These bites were not taken in the same way by the woman and the man. The man was not deceived when he listened to the serpent's words. Tempted by the words of Satan, the man desired to be like God. He decided he was not willing to

21

obey God's words. He rebelled against God's will when he took his bite.

In the Bible, a distinction is drawn between first- and second-degree sin. For example, later, when the people of Israel occupied the Promised Land, God set apart six Cities of Refuge (Numbers 35:11). These were for those who had killed people but were not first-degree, pre-meditated murderers. As second-degree sinners they were punished. They had to flee their homes to escape the avengers and live in a City of Refuge. But, they were spared swift execution which was reserved for those who had willfully committed murder.

Jesus taught this distinction. He said there would be a difference between the kind of punishment given to those who purposely disobeyed and those who did not (Luke 12:47-48).

In the Garden of Eden, both took a bite of the fruit from the tree of the knowledge of good and evil. They ate the forbidden fruit and died.

The woman was deceived by Satan into taking her bite (1 Timothy 2:14b, 2 Corinthians 11:3). **Her bite was "of the second degree."**

The man was not deceived when Satan twisted God's words. But he was tempted when Satan suggested that they had not yet become "like God."

The man desired to know good and evil, to be "like God." He willfully disobeyed God when he took his bite (1 Timothy 2:14a). **His bite was "of the first degree."**

Her bite was of the "second degree."
His bite was of the "first degree."

What happened? Satan in the serpent had set out to murder the woman and the man! Satan was an evil rebel against God and presumed to take God's place over them and tell them what to do. Were Satan's words lies? Yes!

Both of them already were fully in God's image and like-ness. Both already walked with God. They were blameless, naked, and unashamed. They had been blessed by God.

After eating, they both knew good and evil. They saw past their nakedness and were ashamed. Their eyes had been "opened" but now they saw the terrible changes that had happened to their unity with each other and to their relation-ship with God.

They used fig leaves to try to cover themselves from each other! Then, when God approached, they ran the other way and tried to hide themselves from God!

God approached in the cool of the day, called out and then questioned the two who each took a bite. God did not ask Satan in the serpent to speak.

God and the man (Genesis 3:8-12). When God called, the man answered as if the woman wasn't there at all. He spoke only of himself: "*I* heard" — "*I* was afraid" — "*I* was naked" — "*I* hid."

God asked the man to reveal two facts, "Who told you...?" and "Did you eat...?" The man's evil response revealed many things about the man, and he didn't answer either one of God's questions!

There had been three at the tree. Two of them, the man and Satan in the serpent, were rebels.

As a rebel against God, the man didn't tell about the strange voice from the serpent and what lies it had said. The man didn't confess that no one had told him he was naked, but that he saw differently now with his own eyes.

Instead, the man dared to judge God! He blamed God and the woman as being responsible for the evil thing he himself had done. He said, "The woman *you* put here to be with me, *she* gave me some fruit from the tree, and I ate it."

God's command to not eat from that tree had been deadly serious. He ate and, as a result, he had died!

Physically, he had become mortal. The man's intimate relationship with God was broken. So was his unity with the woman. The results of death and rebellion had already begun to show themselves in the man.

God and the woman (Genesis 3:13). God asked the woman, "What have you done?" She answered God in a very different way from the man.

She was deceived no longer. She saw clearly what had happened. In her wisdom, she recognized evil and said, "The serpent deceived me, and I ate."

She unmasked the serpent as the source of her deception. And she confessed what she did when she was deceived — "I ate."

Did she rebel against God along with Satan as the man had just done? Did she blame the man with her? No. Did she accuse God? No.

***

Word patterns. What happened in the Garden of Eden was described in Genesis in two "languages" at the same time: in the "language" of word meanings and in the "language" of word patterns. Both the words and their placement together in patterns told how God responded to the three at the tree.

To illustrate this kind of communication, here are words that have their own meaning that are placed in the order of a word pattern that also has meaning:

On the top was **the head**.
The feet were *at the bottom*.

According to the meaning of the words, the head was on the top and the feet were at the bottom. In addition, the word pattern showed the placement of the head and the feet by using the words top and bottom at the beginning and at the end of the pattern.

This way of communicating in two ways — word meaning and word pattern — may seem unusual in some languages. But this was familiar in Old Testament Hebrew and communicated in a clear way. Both Hebrew word patterns and Hebrew word meanings were used in Genesis 2:4-3:24 to communicate what was said about life and death in the Garden of Eden.

***

God's words to Satan in the serpent (Genesis 3:14-15). God's words to the Satan in the serpent in Genesis 3:14-15 were organized in a word pattern. God did not ask Satan to speak. God already knew about the evil angel who had rebelled and desired to take God's place.

God acted on the woman's truthful words. Satan had lied to her and deceived her. God's words began by building on what the woman had said, *"Because* you did this...."

God cursed the serpent, whose body Satan used, and changed it forever. The serpent would crawl on its belly. It would not be upright like the woman and the man. It would eat the dust the man was made of. It also would die, bringing an end to its days.

Next, God told Satan that the war he had started with the woman was not over. It would continue between them and include Satan's seed and the woman's seed.

God looked ahead and saw that, like a serpent, Satan would strike the heel of her seed. But, God promised that the woman's seed would crush the serpent's head!

Here was a mystery that was revealed with the conception of Jesus by the Holy Spirit. God himself would take part with the woman in this war and crush the head of the serpent-angel through her seed, Jesus Christ!

There in the Garden of Eden, the woman could look forward by faith to coming victory. Outside of Eden, anyone who had faith in God's promised victory of the woman's seed over Satan would be invited to eat from the tree of life forever (Revelation 2:7, 22:1-21).

God's words to the man (Genesis 3:17-19). God's words to the man were organized in the same word pattern as the words to the rebellious serpent-angel. This showed that the man's behavior was like Satan's behavior! But God's words to the woman were not organized the same way at all (Genesis 3:16).

The man had heard the woman describe to God what her enemy, the serpent, had done. The man had heard when God promised Satan that the war he had started would continue until the seed of the woman crushed the serpent-angel.

What had the man done? At the tree, the man had judged God's words to be not good. He had rebelled against God. He had followed the evil words of the Liar.

Afterwards, did the man tell any of that to God? No. The man lied about who he really had listened to and rebelliously blamed God!

When God spoke to the man, God used the man's own words against him. God repeated who the man had blamed — "the *woman*" and "*you*." God said, "Because you have listened to the voice of your *wife*, and have eaten from the tree about which *I* commanded you, saying, 'You shall not eat from it,' *cursed is the ground* because of you!"

What did God do? *God cursed the ground* — but not him. God cursed the ground because of the man. But, God did not curse the man. What restraint! What mercy!

**God cursed the serpent and the ground.
God did not curse the women or the man.**

Next, God taught the man the bad news about life and death. God would chase the man out of the Garden and explained things to the man from that point of view.

The man would experience "sorrowful-toil" (*'itsebon*) as he struggled to grow food from the ground which God had cursed because of him. Food would not be easy to raise. Thorns and thistles would come from the cursed ground and make the work harder.

"Sorrowful-toil" was a Hebrew word only used three times in the Bible (Genesis 3:17, 3:16 and 5:29). Each time, this "sorrowful-toil" came from working the ground that God cursed because of the man.

The word "sorrowful-toil" sounded very much like the word "tree" in Hebrew. It brought to mind the fruit he had eaten from the tree of the knowledge of good and evil.

Every drop of sweat that fell from the tip of the man's nose and into the dust was to remind him of the good work he had been given to do in the Garden of Eden, where he lived in perfect relationship with God, his Creator, and with the woman, his companion.

God told the man that his days in his body would come to an end. His body would die. God explained that his body was formed from the dust of the ground and to the dust his body would return (Genesis 3:19).

God's eleven words to the woman (Genesis 3:16).
God's words to the woman were not arranged in same pattern used with the serpent-angel and with the man. Her case was different from the two rebels. Her situation was unlike theirs.

God's words to her were not all about bad news. Instead, God spoke to her of good news and bad news.

27

God's words to the woman took only eleven Hebrew words. Some of these were common words. Some were very rare words. A look at each word is needed in order to think again about the meaning of the whole verse.

Words 1-4. Here are the first four Hebrew words in Line 1 of Genesis 3:16 that came after the words of introduction, "God said to-the-woman":

(word 1) Multiplying (word 2) I-will-multiply
(word 3) your-sorrowful-toil
(word 4) and-your-conception.

God said to the woman that two things (words 3 and 4) would be multiplied, or would surely come to pass. God said she would experience "sorrowful-toil" (*'itsebon*). And God said she would experience "conception" (*heron*).

Words 1 and 2 — "to multiply." The verb, to-multiply, used in words 1 and 2 was familiar to the woman. She had heard it on Day 6 when God blessed her and her husband and said to them, "Be fruitful and multiply, and fill the earth ..." (Genesis 1:28).

In Genesis 3:16, this action word was repeated in a way which spoke of things that were sure to come to pass. Most translations get the idea across in the English phrase, "I will surely multiply."

To repeat "to multiply" in this way was done only three times in the Old Testament (Genesis 3:16, 16:10, 22:17). Each time these words came from God. Each time the word "seed" was used along with them.

"Seed" was a meaningful word. It spoke of *a* seed, but it contained within it the possibility of *many* seeds, or descendants. For example, God made this promise after he blessed Abraham, "I will surely multiply your seed ... and in your seed all the nations of the earth shall be blessed, because you have obeyed my voice" (Genesis 22:17).

Word 3 — "sorrowful-toil." God told the woman she would experience two things. She would have (word 3) "sorrowful-toil" and (word 4) "conception."

The man would be told about "sorrowful-toil" in the next verse, in Genesis in 3:17. They would experience the same "sorrowful-toil." The single cause of it would be God's curse on the ground because of the man.

All food would have to come from the cursed soil. It would be this "sorrowful-toil" the woman and the man would experience. It had to do with raising food.

When God told the woman she would experience "sorrowful-toil" the earth had not yet been cursed. This prophecy told what would happen but not what would cause it to happen.

The word "sorrowful-toil" (*'itsebon*) was a very rare word. In addition to God's prediction of it to the woman in Genesis 3:16 and God's announcement of it to the man in Genesis 3:17, it was used in Genesis 5:29. In Genesis 5:29 its meaning was the same.

When the parents of newborn Noah named him, they expressed their hope that life would be better because of this child. They hoped he would provide them relief from the "sorrowful-toil" they were experiencing as the result of the curse on the soil. They "… called his name Noah, saying, 'This one will comfort us concerning our work and the sorrowful-toil of our hands, because of the ground which the Lord has cursed.'"

This was not just any kind of work. The English words "work" or "toil" are not nearly as precise as the Hebrew word. It was a very specific kind of toil, a "sorrowful-toil." It meant: "the-sorrowful-toil-which-results-from-God's-curse-on-the-soil."

This is the bad news God announced to the woman. She would have "sorrowful-toil."

Word 4 — "conception." The woman had heard God tell Satan in the serpent about her "seed" (Genesis 3:15). In Genesis 3:16, God spoke to her directly about her seed. The meaningful word "conception" was used for seed.

Many people have missed the connection of the promise of "seed" in verse 15 with "conception" in verse 16. To conceive and have seed or descendants was big news! It was a look into the woman's future. It was also a look into victory over her enemy!

Sadly, many translations make it look as if God's first words to the woman in Genesis 3:16 had all bad news, or even something like a curse, for the woman. Not so!

From our place in history, it is possible to see the whole line of descendants who were conceived from the first woman down to Mary, the virgin who conceived by the Holy Spirit (Luke 3:23-38, Galatians 3:16). Mary's child Jesus was the Seed to crush the serpent's head!

Because most modern translations do not use the word "conception," another important truth from the Garden of Eden is missed. There is no question of when human life begins when Genesis 3:16 is translated correctly. Human life begins at conception!

What about the translations of Genesis 3:16 that have said that God spoke about "pain in childbirth?" They are incorrect.

God did not speak about "childbirth" in these first four Hebrew words to the woman. God spoke of "conception." Conception took place nine months before childbirth!

God did not speak to the woman about "pain." God spoke to her about the "sorrowful-toil" that would be involved in raising crops from the cursed ground.

There is nothing about "pain in childbirth" in the first four Hebrew words of Genesis 3:16. This must be kept in mind in order to clearly understand the rest of God's words to the woman in Genesis 3:16.

Words 5-11. In the next seven Hebrew words in Genesis 3:16, words 5 through 11, God told the woman other important things. God explained what life would be like after sin and death at the tree.

(word 5) With-effort (6) you-will-bring-forth (7) children
(word 8) Your-desire [is] (9) for-your-husband
(word 10) But-he (11) will-rule-over-you

Words 5-7. With *these* words, not before, God told her about childbirth. God explained that, as a mother with a mortal body that was subject to pain and death, she would give birth with "effort." The word "effort" (*'etsev*) was not a word reserved for childbearing. It was used in other places in the Bible for various types of effort.

God did not curse the woman nor did God change her childbearing with these words. Nowhere in God's eleven words to the woman was the Hebrew word "curse" used.

The news that childbearing would involve "effort" was said on the way to glad news, because next God spoke of "children." She would bear more than just one child! God's commandment of Day 6 to be fruitful parents and fill the earth with children was still in effect!

Would the first of her children crush Satan? There was drama for her as she looked forward to the first child she would conceive!

Words 8-11. Next, God explained to the woman what had happened to her relationship with the man. There was glad news and sad news.

In words 8 and 9, God spoke about what was in her heart — it had not changed. They were newlyweds. They had desired each other. Ah, love! God confirmed that her "desire" was "for her husband" as it had been before.

She had not rebelled like the man and taken the side of the serpent. Her words to God were not twisted like theirs were. She had not blamed the man. Her desire for him was not twisted either.

Her desire was good and natural. The word "desire" of one lover for another was used in the Bible only one other time. It was a good desire (Song of Solomon 7:11).

In words 10 and 11, God explained the sad news about the change in her husband. God explained to the woman the man was not like he was when God brought them together. The man had rejected his good relationship with God and had presumed to rule in God's place!

The man also had rejected her. He had turned against the woman by blaming her along with God for his sin (Genesis 3:12).

God alone had the right to rule over the woman, just as it was right for God to rule over the man. God warned the woman that the man who had presumed to rule over himself desired to take the place of God again — to rule over her!

For the man to impose this on the woman was not good, it was evil. It is evil for anyone to take the place of God!

End of Eden (Genesis 3:20-24)

What had happened? God had looked into the man's heart and had warned the woman of what the man desired to do. Then, God had judged the man and condemned him to a limited lifetime in the fields with a final return to the dust.

The man responded (Genesis 3:20). What happened next? Did the man turn from his rebellious ways and return to God letting God rule over him? He did not.

The man rejected God's will again in his very first words after God's judgment. The man did to the woman something he had done to the animals (Genesis 2:19-20)! He called her with a name of his choice.

God had not told the man to give a name to the other human being. God had already given them a name. God had named both of them *adam* (Genesis 5): as in Mr. and Mrs. Adam.

The man went off on his own way. He took the name "Adam" for himself alone and gave the woman a different name.

On Day 6, God had told them both to rule over all the other living beings on earth. By naming her in this way, the man acted as if he ruled over her! Did this please God?

God had just talked to him about turning into dust in death. Did the man who was dying name her "Eve," which means "living," to point out she was his opposite? Was this another act of defiance and separation by the man?

The woman was not known by the name "Eve" until the man made it up. No verses in Genesis 1:1-3:19 used the name Eve. Not even once. For this reason, in this commentary, the name "Eve" was not used prior to Genesis 3:20.

God acted (Genesis 3:21-24). God covered the shame of the man and the woman. No fig leaves could do the job! It took animal skins obtained by the shedding of blood. How much of this did they understand? Later, their son Abel knew that to offer a blood sacrifice was the right thing to do (Genesis 4:4).

Then, God drove Adam out of the garden! He was no longer allowed to eat from the tree of life. Outside of the Garden, the man had only the dust of the ground he was made of. From that dust he was to raise his own food.

God placed an angelic guard at the tree of life in case the man dared to disobey again! No one would be able to eat its fruit.

Outside of Eden (Genesis 4-5)

Genesis 1 and 2 told how God acted in creation and love. Genesis 3 told how Satan acted in evil rebellion and told lies to lead the woman and man to their death. Nevertheless, the Lord continued a relationship with Adam and Eve, with their children and with their descendants as recorded in Genesis 4-5.

Children. Cain, the first child conceived by Eve with Adam, was the first one who could possibly fulfill the promise by the Lord of the "seed" who would crush the head of the serpent. Eve gave the Lord the credit for his conception and birth (Genesis 4:1).

Abel, a second child, fulfilled the Lord's word to her that she would bear more than one child, or "children." A third child would be born, Seth. And, many more boys and girls were born as Adam and Eve were fruitful and multiplied and began to fill the earth with their children.

Cain and Abel grew up into adults. Abel was a keeper of flocks. Cain was a tiller of the ground (Genesis 4:2). Everyone ate fruit and grains. No blood was shed to kill animals for food (Genesis 1:29-30).

In Genesis 4:1-16, the history was told of Adam and Eve and their first two sons. Then, starting with Genesis 4:17 two lines of descendants were traced.

One line of descendants, from Cain, was made up of rebellious persons and their shameful acts (Genesis 4:17-23). The other line of descendants, from Seth, was made up of godly persons and their acts of faith (Genesis 4:25-5:32).

Cain. Some time after their births outside of Eden, Cain and Abel brought sacrifices to God. Cain offered the fruit of the ground to God. Abel offered a blood sacrifice from the first-born animals he raised. God accepted Abel and his offering, but God did not accept Cain and his gift (Genesis 4:4-5).

After that, Cain knew what kind of sacrifice to offer to please God. It was the kind of offering Abel had made to God. But Cain was angry with God and very unhappy.

God reached out to Cain. God told him he could still do what was right. God warned Cain that he was very close to being consumed by sin (Genesis 4:6-7). What loving instruction! What a timely warning! What clear direction!

But, Cain was unwilling to be obedient to the will of God. He rebelled against God's word and, in his heart, walked his own rebellious path.

Cain invited his brother, Abel, to go with him into his fields. Able went with him. But Cain, overcome by sin, overpowered his brother and killed him. And the cursed ground soaked up the blood of his murdered brother!

God confronted and judged Cain (Genesis 4:10-16). God cursed Cain to never again be a fruitful tiller of the ground. He would have to be a wanderer instead.

But Cain did not turn back to God. Cain even refused to be a wanderer and began to build a city which he named after his son Enoch.

What happened to Cain's evil descendants was told in Genesis 4:17-24. By the time of the seventh generation, evil Lamech became a murderer of two men and married two wives! He was proud and defiant. This was the first line of descendants listed in the pattern of Genesis 4-5.

Seth. In Genesis 4:25-5:32, the line of Seth was described. Seth was the third child of Adam and Eve. He was righteous as Abel had been. His descendants worshipped God.

By the time of the seventh generation, an Enoch in the family of Seth was born. He became the father of Methuselah. Unlike the great sinner, Lamech, Enoch pleased God. He walked with God to the point that God spared him from death!

Two generations later, Noah was born. He walked with God and was blameless among the people of his generation.

***

35

Share your thinking: Discussion questions on Chapter 1 of
Women & Men.

With each answer, note the verse, or verses, where it was
found.

1. The man and the woman were made in whose image and
   likeness?

2. Who was told to rule over all living things?

3. What was the difference between the way the woman
   and the man took a bite of the fruit?

4. How did they respond differently to God's questions?

5. God gave good news to the woman that was bad news to
   Satan in the serpent. What was it?

6. Did God curse the man or the woman?

7. Did the curse on the ground affect the woman? The
   man?

8. Which is better according to Genesis 1-2 – to be a man
   or a woman? Is either one better?

9. Outside of Eden, did God withdraw from the woman
   and the man and their children?

10. Are you rebellious like Satan and Adam, or are you at
    peace with God like Abel?

Chapter Two

Together with Christ
in the Church

From the Garden to the Church. (Genesis - Acts)

In the beginning, God Three-in-One created everything and then made the man and the woman in his image and likeness. Each one knew God. God brought the woman and the man together into a remarkable "one-flesh" relationship, united in marriage (Genesis 2:24-25). They were naked and not ashamed before each other or before God who spoke with them. Everything was very good.

Satan rebelled against God. He came in a serpent and attacked the first two humans in the Garden of Eden. Satan-in-the-serpent, the murderer and liar, got each one to take a bite of the tree of the knowledge of good and evil. They died! They covered themselves, then hid from God (Genesis 3:1-8).

How did God respond to the two bites taken by the woman and the man? How did God respond to the answer each one gave to God's questions?

God promised conception for the woman. Her "seed" would crush Satan's head.

God cursed the ground because of the man but God did not curse either the woman or the man. God drove the man from the Garden of Eden and blocked the way to the tree of life. The man and the woman would have sorrowful toil as they worked the cursed earth outside of the Garden of Eden (Genesis 3:9-24).

The Old Testament. The way to reconciliation with God was clear to the children of Adam and Eve. Sin resulted in death. Forgiveness of sin was possible through the death of an acceptable substitute. Abel took that way when he offered a lamb of sacrifice. Cain rejected it.

The children of Seth down to Noah offered acceptable sacrifices. The children of Cain did not.

Through the years, from Noah to Abraham to Moses to the prophets, God continued to seek and receive anyone who got forgiveness for their sins. Moses was told by God to set up the Tabernacle where sacrifices were offered. God visibly was present at the Tabernacle, and later at the Temple built by Solomon, King David's son.

As time passed, God's revealed word was written down in the thirty nine historical, prophetic and poetic books of the Old Testament. They were filled with the history of the descendants of the woman and the man from the Garden of Eden. The Psalms and the other poetic books were filled with praise for God and with teaching on how to live for God. The books of the prophets revealed more of God's will and God's plan.

The New Testament. The first five books of the New Testament told about the coming, earthly ministry and ascension of Jesus, and about the ministry of the Holy Spirit through the first generation of the church. During this time, instructions on how to live for Christ were written down and sent to groups of believers. Finally, John, the youngest one of the Twelve who had walked with Jesus, received and wrote down the Revelation, the last book of the Bible.

John the Baptist was a prophet. His work was to prepare the way for the promised Seed of the woman (Luke 3:1-18). John the Baptist preached, "I baptize you with water, but he will baptize you with the Holy Spirit" (Mark 1:8).

At that time Jesus came from Nazareth in Galilee and was baptized by John in the Jordan. As Jesus was coming up out of the water, he saw heaven being torn open and the Spirit descending on him like a dove. And a voice came from heaven: "You are my Son, whom I love; with you I am well pleased." (Mark 1:9-11)

The Holy Spirit led Jesus into the wild desert to be tempted. There, Satan tried to cause Jesus to sin. The results were not the same as in the Garden of Eden. Jesus was not deceived nor did he rebel against God. Satan attacked Jesus three ways.

1. Eat something God never intended to be eaten!
2. Risk yourself and defy certain death!
3. Follow me and rule right now!

All three times, Jesus quoted God's words and obeyed God. He did not follow Satan's murderous lies (Luke 4:1-13).

Then, by his public miracles and teaching, Jesus showed that he was the promised "seed." He fulfilled more than 300 prophecies that were written about him throughout the Old Testament.

He came to die for the sins of the world. As that day approached, Jesus told those who walked with him that though he would no longer walk beside them, the Spirit would be in them (John 14:26, 20:22, Acts 1:8-15, 1 Corinthians 3:16, 6:19, 1 John 4:13-15).

He was condemned to death, even though he was blameless. Jesus died on the cross as a substitute. He paid the penalty of death for all sinners. He was buried. On the third day he rose from the dead, the firstborn of all who receive everlasting life (Revelation 1:5-6, Hebrews 2:14-15)!

That day, and over a period of forty days, Jesus met with his disciples, or messengers, and his other followers and explained the Old Testament to them. He gave orders to tell all peoples the Good News of salvation through the blood he shed on the cross.

On one of these occasions Jesus said, "All authority in heaven and on earth has been given to me. Therefore go and make disciples of all peoples, baptizing them in the name of the Father and of the Son and of the Holy Spirit, and teaching them to obey everything I have commanded you. Surely I am with you always, to the very end of the age" (Matthew 28:18-20).

Jesus promised the power of the Spirit to spread the Good News in Jerusalem, Judea, Samaria and to the ends of the earth (Luke 24:44-49, Matthew 28:19-20, Acts 1:2-8, 2:1-41). Then, he ascended to heaven (Acts 1:9, Hebrews 10:12).

The church — Jesus and his followers united. After Jesus ascended to heaven, men and women followers of his began meeting together. There were about one hundred and twenty of them (Acts 1:15). Ten days later, the Holy Spirit visibly came upon them and gave each one the power to tell the Good News of Christ to the many thousands of Jews who had come to the city of Jerusalem. These Jews came from many nations to celebrate the Feast of First Fruits, or Pentecost (1 Kings 8:10-11, Acts 2:1-4, 17-18).

Those who became followers of Jesus were baptized in the name of the Father, and of the Son, and of the Holy Spirit, as Jesus had instructed (Matthew 28:19). Followers of Jesus believed in the covering of their sins by the blood of the Savior. A "follower" was "born of the Spirit" (John 3:3, 5-8). The number of new followers added that day was about 3,000 (Acts 2:38, 41).

They worshipped together in the Temple. They gathered together regularly in homes, continually devoting themselves to the teaching of the messengers and to fellowship, to the breaking of bread, and to prayer (Acts 2:42).

What teaching? The messengers of Jesus taught what Jesus had explained to them about the Old Testament during his ministry and after his resurrection (Luke 24:44-45). From personal experience they taught about the events in the life of Jesus. They had heard the public preaching and private teaching of Jesus and they repeated his words.

As Jesus had promised, the Holy Spirit taught them and reminded them of "everything I have told you" (John 14:26). Over time, the twenty-seven books of the New Testament were written down. They were God's inspiration: "All Scripture is God-breathed and is useful for teaching, rebuking, correcting and training in righteousness, so that all God's people may be thoroughly equipped for every good work" (2 Timothy 3:16-17, TNIV).

The four Gospels and the book of Acts told about the events and words of Jesus and the first generation of followers of Jesus. The rest of the books of the New Testament were written down as letters to be delivered to others far away.

The twenty-two letters, from Romans to Revelation, gave teaching and advice. These letters were not organized as stories that included events and words. Instead they were organized by ideas grouped in word patterns.

Over time, those who had been with Jesus had all passed away. But, by then, the twenty-seven books of the New Testament had been written by them and others who were inspired by the Spirit.

The followers of Jesus, who were born of the Spirit with everlasting life, received spiritual gifts (1 Corinthians 12:7, Romans 12:4-8). Some followers received the gift of serving the other followers, to build them up (Ephesians 4:11-12). The result among all followers was growth "until we all reach unity in the faith and in the knowledge of the Son of God and become mature, attaining to the whole measure of the fullness of Christ" (Ephesians 4:13).

Every follower played an important part in the life and health of the whole body of Christ (1 Corinthians 12:7). This included telling the good news to everyone, even to the ends of the earth (Romans 10:13-15, Matthew 28:20, Acts 1:8).

Paul. When the number of followers of Jesus in Jerusalem first began to grow, the religious leaders, who hated Jesus, hated them as well. One of the followers, Stephen, who was full of the power of the Holy Spirit, was tried and put to death for his teaching about Jesus!

That day, a violent persecution broke out against the followers, and most of them fled the city. They were scattered to many lands.

In each place where they found themselves, they told others the Good News of Jesus Christ. Soon, more and more followers of Jesus were meeting together in many places near and far (Acts 7:51-8:4, 9:26-31).

Saul of Tarsus was a scholar who carefully followed the religious rules and regulations he had learned. But, this did not help him walk with God. He was involved in the killing of Stephen.

He persecuted the followers of Jesus in Jerusalem and beyond. Later, he called himself the "worst of sinners" (1 Timothy 1:15).

But, Jesus appeared to him. Jesus caused him to see how wrong he was. Saul turned from his sin and became a follower of Jesus (Acts 9:3-20).

Jesus gave him the assignment to serve as his special messenger outside of Israel, especially to the non-Jews of the Roman Empire. Paul, along with his companions, was sent out by the Holy Spirit from the church at Antioch and took the message of the Good News of Christ to many Roman cities and the neighboring countryside (Acts 13-14).

Paul carefully explained the "mystery." The word "mystery" described something that was not fully understood until it was fulfilled and revealed by God.

Jesus Christ was born in Bethlehem of a virgin. As promised in the Garden of Eden, Jesus was the seed of God and a woman! He was wounded on the cross and gave up his life, But he rose from the dead and triumphed over death. He offered everlasting life to anyone who accepted his death for their sins, turned from their shameful ways and followed him. Paul called this "the revelation of the mystery hidden for long ages past, but now revealed" (Romans 16:25-26).

Ephesians. At one point, Paul spent several years teaching in the major city of Ephesus (Acts 19:8-10). Later, Paul wrote a letter and sent it to the followers of Jesus in the region of Ephesus. In it, he explained that God had given him the responsibility to make known the previously hidden "mystery" of Christ (Ephesians 3:1-9):

... by revelation there was made known to me the mystery ... of Christ, which in other generations was not made known .... which for ages has been hidden in God who created all things ....

One in Christ. In an earlier letter to a different group of followers of Jesus, Paul told them that they were all united in Christ Jesus. "There is neither Jew nor Greek, slave nor free, male nor female, for you are all one in Christ Jesus" (Galatians 3:28).

In his Letter to the Ephesians, Paul explained that every follower, whether Jew or non-Jew, was joined together with every other follower in three ways. The second way was a specially important word picture.

In reading this, then, you will be able to understand my insight ... that the non-Jews should be **joint-heirs** and a **joint-body** and **joint-sharers** of the promise in Christ Jesus through the Gospel. (Ephesians 3:4-6)

To picture a joint-body, it is helpful to look at the body of an ant. The ant has a three-part joint-body with (1) a head, (2) a thorax and (3) an abdomen. No one part alone is the body. Each part works together with the others to form one joint-body.

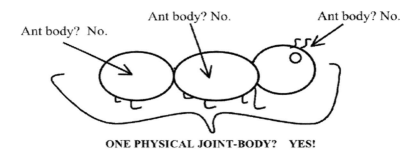

Ant body? No.   Ant body? No.   Ant body? No.

ONE PHYSICAL JOINT-BODY?   YES!

Human beings have a two-part joint-body with (1) a head and (2) a torso, or trunk. Neither part alone is the body. As the parts work jointly together, the whole body prospers.

In Ephesians 4, Paul again used the word picture of a joint-body. It included the two parts that together make up the body of Christ — (1) the followers of Jesus plus (2) Jesus himself: "... we may grow into him ... the head, Christ, of whom all the body ... grows and builds itself up in love, as each part does its work" (Ephesians 4:15-16).

In English, the word "body" can be confusing. It may include both the head and the trunk, or torso. But the English word "body" may refer only to the trunk and not include the head.

In some languages, there is a different word that refers to both the head and trunk together. Such a word completes the image and makes it all clear. But the limitations of the words used in English has led to a confusion of trunks and heads.

Paul's word picture showed how followers and Christ, together, form one united body. The "body of Christ" was a two-part joint-body. This "body" included followers and Christ himself. One part, plus one part, equaled one whole joint-body.

Paul's words in Ephesians 4:15-16 did not refer to a literal body. It was a simple word picture — followers and Christ together make up one joint-body.

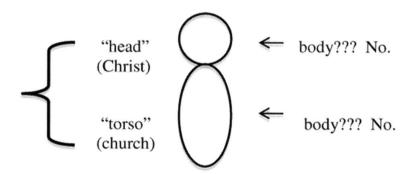

ONE SPIRITUAL JOINT-BODY? YES!

Paul used this word picture of a joint-body in Ephesians and in his other letters. Each time, he used it to picture a *united* body (Romans 12:5, 1 Corinthians 11:3, 12:12-27, Ephesians 1:22, 4:11-13, 5:23, 31-32, Colossians 1:18, 2:19).

***

Many of the first readers of Ephesians were familiar with the Hebrew word patterns that Paul integrated into his writing style. It is very helpful whenever possible to look into Ephesians with an eye to the patterns that were used to organize it. Here are some very important ones from the second half of Ephesians.

1. In the second half of Ephesians six passages began with the Greek words "therefore" and "walk." The last one was slightly different. It said "therefore" and "stand."

Ephesians 4:1-16 — "Therefore" "walk" in a worthy manner

Ephesians 4:17-32 — "Therefore" "walk" not in confusion

Ephesians 5:1-6 — "Therefore" "walk" in love

Ephesians 5:7-14 — "Therefore" "walk" as children of light

Ephesians 5:15-6:9 — "Therefore" "walk" very carefully

Ephesians 6:10-20 — "Therefore" "stand" against the devil

2. The fifth passage and sixth passage corresponded roughly to Genesis chapters two and three. These chapters in Genesis often have been labeled "Creation" and "Fall." But a closer look revealed that chapter three of Genesis was not about a "Fall" but about an "Attack" and its aftermath. The two passages of Ephesians 5:15-6:9 and 6:10-18 can be similarly labeled "New Creation" and "Defense against Attack."

Paul revealed that the unity of Christ and the church was better even than the unity of the man and woman and God in the Garden of Eden. Followers of Jesus who made up the church were filled with the Spirit of Christ. And, when attacked by Satan, they could successfully stand against his attacks!

3. There were three groups of actions strung together in Ephesians 5:15-6:9. These three groups had four parts each. They followed the Hebrew word pattern of grouping together "three parts plus a fourth part" as in Proverbs 30:18-19. Paul took the fourth part of each group of actions and used the next group of actions to explain it more fully.

***

Christ and the church and the acts of the Spirit (Eph 5:15-6:9)
To tell the important story of the unity of Christ and his followers, Paul started the fifth passage of the second half of Ephesians with strong words. Paul wrote, "*See to it* that you walk *very* carefully."

1. **"Careful walking."** In Group One (Ephesians 5:15b-18), Paul contrasted three actions *not* to do with three actions *to* do. The fourth contrasting actions were different from the first three. The last action was not something *to do* but something *to let the Spirit do*!

Don't be unwise walkers! / Be wise walkers! (5:15b)
Don't be thoughtless! / Make the most of your time! (5:16)
Don't be foolish! / Understand the will of the Lord! (5:17)
Don't be controlled by wine! / **Be filled with the Spirit!** (5:18)

Someone who was "drunk" was not in control of himself. He was controlled by all the wine that was in him. In every follower of Christ was the Spirit of Christ (Romans 8:5-14). Paul told followers always to let the Spirit be in control of them. Being controlled by wine led to certain acts. Being controlled by the Spirit led to certain acts as well.

Being controlled by wine led to certain actions. Being controlled by the Spirit led to certain actions.

The Ephesian followers knew about the Holy Spirit. Jesus had sent the Spirit to be in every follower after he went up to heaven.

In the city of Jerusalem on the Day of Pentecost two different things happened. The first happened to about 120 men and women. These followers were meeting together in the upper room that morning. The Spirit came and gave them power to do something. They received power to preach the Good News in many languages. So they started to preach to those around them!

The second thing happened to the thousands who responded to their preaching. They heard, "Repent and be baptized, every one of you, in the name of Jesus Christ for the forgiveness of your sins." Thousands of them did so and received the gift of the Holy Spirit (Acts 2; 4:29, 31). This is what Jesus called being "born again" and "born of the Spirit" (John 3:3-8).

The Ephesians who received Paul's letter knew about this. They, too, had been born of the Spirit when they first believed.

2. "Acts of the Spirit." In Group Two (Ephesians 5:18b-21), the Holy Spirit produced acts, or works, in the followers of Jesus. Two were "vertical" and directed toward God — the second and third acts in verses 19b and 20. Two were "horizontal" and directed to one another — the first and fourth acts in verses 19a and 21. The fourth one was developed further in the third group where two more acts were added.

There was also an additional act of the Spirit. It was described at the end of the sixth passage in Ephesians 6:18.

All of these acts were practical activities that followers of Jesus could do and that others could see. They were the result of being filled by the Holy Spirit.

The first action was — Speaking to one another in psalms and hymns and spiritual songs (5:19a). This action was "horizontal" or directed toward other followers. What kind of speaking was this? Colossians 3:16 used the action words "teaching and encouraging" for "speaking" in a parallel passage.

Teaching and encouraging one another was a result of the influence of the Holy Spirit in the followers of Jesus. All followers — mature and newborn, adult and child, woman and man, boy and girl — were led by the Spirit to encourage one another with God's words. Paul used the examples of the words of psalms, hymns and spiritual songs.

There were many psalms, hymns and spiritual songs recorded, or referred to, in the Bible. The Book of Psalms had 150 of them. After the last supper, Jesus and the twelve sang a hymn and left the upper room (Matthew 26:30). Paul and Silas sang hymns the night they were in jail (Acts 16:25). Songs were sung by Moses, Miriam, and others (Exodus 21:1-21, Deuteronomy 32:1-47, 1 Corinthians 14:15).

The psalms, hymns and spiritual songs taught what to do. They taught what not to do. They taught what to know and think about. They taught wisdom. They praised God.

Speaking, or teaching and encouraging, one another in this way did not require followers to be literate and meet in a Bible study, as such. Memorizing the words from psalms, hymns and spiritual songs, and passing along their words was sufficient.

The majority of people around the world cannot, or do not, read. But they can teach and encourage one another with the words of psalms, hymns and spiritual songs.

Paul already had written that "speaking the truth in love … makes the body grow so that it builds itself up in love" (Ephesians 4:15-16). According to Ephesians 5:19a, every follower in the church was to be involved in this speaking to one another. The result of this action among the followers was growth "until we all reach unity in the faith and in the knowledge of the Son of God and become mature, attaining to the whole measure of the fullness of Christ" (Ephesians 4:13).

The second ongoing action was directed "vertically" to God — Singing and making music in your heart to the Lord (5:19b). Followers of Jesus did this because of his Spirit within them. But, those who were drunk and controlled by wine sang very different songs and in a very different way.

The third ongoing action was also "vertical" — Thanking always God the Father for everything (5:20). This was to be done in the name of Jesus.

The fourth ongoing action was the second one that was "horizontal" — Submitting yourselves one to another, in respect of Christ (5:21).

What were they to submit to? First of all, they were submitting themselves to the biblical teaching and encouragement they heard from one another (Ephesians 5:19a, 21)!

Believers were submitting themselves to the teaching and encouragement of one another!

This fourth action resulted from being filled with the Spirit. It was a major point in Paul's teaching.

Paul wrote these words, inspired by God, after many years of starting new churches and returning to teach and correct the followers of Jesus in these churches. He knew how important it was for everyone to be teaching one another and to be submitting to one another.

The misunderstanding of horizontal speaking and submitting in the church has led to a reduction in teaching and responding to God's Word. The work of the Spirit among his followers is limited when only one person, or just a few, are teaching the others. A basic part in the life of Christians together is for all to teach, all to encourage, all to listen and all to learn.

In Ephesians 5:21, Paul worked very hard to make his meaning clear because "submitting one to another" was a new way to act. It was not the way people submitted outside the church. The common meaning of the action word — "submit-to" — meant that a person who was "under" had to submit-to a person who was "over" them.

But this was not how followers of Jesus were to act. Jesus said that no group of followers was to rule over the others (Matthew 20:25-28).

Paul redefined submitting as it occurred in the Spirit among followers of Jesus. He described their new way of interacting with one another with these words — "Be-submitting-yourselves." This was something followers volunteered to do over and over again. It was the way of life in the Spirit!

To this, Paul added "one-to-another." This completed the meaning. In their shared submitting, each one gave up any idea about being "over" the other one. All were side-by-side!

Paul redefined "submitting" for believers.

Paul used the last three Greek words in verse 21 to show it was something done among followers of Christ. Every other time in the Bible the words "in the-respect of-…" ended with the word "*God*." But not here. In verse 21 Paul ended with the words "in the-respect of-*Christ*."

3. "Christ's examples." In Group Three (Ephesians 5:22-32), Paul explained further how followers of Jesus were to be submitting themselves one to another. He gave examples based on Christ's actions.

Paul began with three side-by-side comparisons. In each comparison, "as Christ" was the second and main part.

As Christ was Savior of the body (church) (5:23b)
As Christ loved and gave himself for the church (5:25b-27)
As Christ loved and cared for the body (church) (5:29-30)

The first three examples of how Christ loved and gave himself for the church led up to the statement of the great mystery of how Christ and the church are united in one joint-body. This fourth part was the high point in the whole passage of Ephesians 5:15-6:9.

Christ and the church are one joint-body (5:31-32)

In the Garden of Eden, the first man and woman were joined by God in the special united relationship of husband and wife (Genesis 2:24-25). In Ephesians 5:31, Paul referred to that relationship in Eden to cast light on the special united spiritual relationship of Christ and the church!

"For this reason a man will leave his father and mother and will commit to his wife, and the two will become one flesh." Here is a great mystery — I am talking about Christ and the church! (Ephesians 5:31-32)

This great revelation, or mystery, was not clearly understood by the disciples when Christ breathed on them (John 20:21-22), and then ascended into heaven a short time later (Acts 1:9-10). It became clearer to them on the Day of Pentecost (Acts 2:32-33).

By the time new followers were gathering together, from Jerusalem to Judea and Samaria to across the Roman Empire, Paul explained it clearly. The great mystery was the revelation of the wonderful relationship of his followers united together with Christ!

The union of the first man and woman in the Garden of Eden was good. But, walking in the union of Christ and the church was even better!

In Ephesians 5:22-30, Paul linked together the three "as Christ" examples. He used the word pattern that was used in Genesis 3:15-17. This word pattern used two actions in three parts — one was in the first example, one was in the third example, and both were used in the middle example.

In the first example Christ gave of himself as savior for the church (5:23b). In the third example Christ loved and cared for the church (29-30). In the middle example Christ did both for the church: "as Christ loved the church and gave himself up for her" (25b).

All followers of Jesus could act in these two ways as well. They could submit themselves to one another first by giving of themselves for one another. They also could submit themselves to one another by loving and caring for one another.

***

Sadly, the context and the content of these verses have been misunderstood. Instead of pointing to Christ's examples of how to treat one another in the body of Christ, this passage has been seen as a passage on marriage. Yet, Paul made his meaning perfectly clear when he wrote in verse 32, "I am talking about Christ and the church."

***

Christ's first example. In Ephesians 5:23, Paul used a joint-body word picture two times. A husband and wife were united as "head" and "trunk" in one complete joint-body. Christ and the church were united as "head" and "trunk" in one complete joint-body. Christ's example was in how he gave of himself, as "savior of the body" (Ephesians 5:23).

Christ's second example. Paul introduced a second action of Christ and added it to the first one. Christ "loved the church," and "gave himself up for her" (verses 25b-27).

Christ's third example. Paul repeated the second action in another way. Christ "nourished and cherished" the church just as a person cared for his own body. Christ did so because believers are members of his body (verses 29-30).

Practical examples. In Ephesians 5:22-32, when Paul presented his four points in a row that had to do with Christ and the church, he also added a parallel set of three examples in verses 22-30. These three examples pictured how Christians were submitting themselves one to another. After verses 31-32, Paul added a second set of three more examples, in Ephesians 5:33-6:9.

1. Three practical examples paired with Christ's examples (5:22-30)
2. Three more practical examples (5:33-6:9)

At the beginning of each of these sets of examples, Paul carefully linked them to Ephesians 5:21. These links were made at verse 22 and at verse 33.

First, Ephesians 5:22 was linked to verse 21 by one action word. Verse 22 had no action word at all in Greek. It only said, "Wives — (*no verb*) — with your own husbands in the Lord."

In the written Greek language, whenever there was a missing action word, as in verse 22, people knew to reach back to the one that had just been used. The action of believers submitting one to another in verse 21 was also the action word for verse 22: "Wives *be submitting one to another* with your husbands, in the Lord."

This made sense. If all believers were to behave this way, it certainly could be practiced between married believers, wives and husbands. Walking together this way in the Spirit pointed to the united relationship of Christ and the church.

Second, Ephesians 5:33 linked back to Ephesians 5:21 in two ways. It began with a linking word and it repeated a key word from verse 21.

The Greek linking word used at the beginning of verse 33 was "to continue." The word "respect" used at the end of verse 33 repeated the word "respect" used in verse 21.

Paul also used links inside of smaller groups of verses and words. These were the same kind of links used in the passage on the Garden of Eden in Genesis 2:4-3:24.

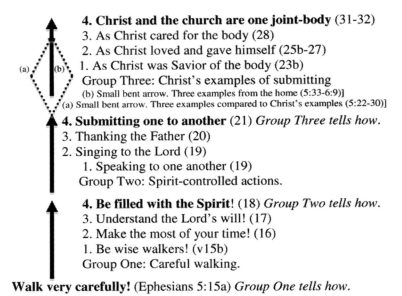

4. Christ and the church are one joint-body (31-32)
3. As Christ cared for the body (28)
2. As Christ loved and gave himself (25b-27)
1. As Christ was Savior of the body (23b)
Group Three: Christ's examples of submitting
(b) Small bent arrow. Three examples from the home (5:33-6:9)]
(a) Small bent arrow. Three examples compared to Christ's examples (5:22-30)]

4. Submitting one to another (21) *Group Three tells how.*
3. Thanking the Father (20)
2. Singing to the Lord (19)
1. Speaking to one another (19)
Group Two: Spirit-controlled actions.

4. Be filled with the Spirit! (18) *Group Two tells how.*
3. Understand the Lord's will! (17)
2. Make the most of your time! (16)
1. Be wise walkers! (v15b)
Group One: Careful walking.

Walk very carefully! (Ephesians 5:15a) *Group One tells how.*

The first three practical examples, in verses 22-30, were linked to verse 21. Then, Paul combined them one by one with Christ's three examples.

In the practical example in verse 22, when Paul used the modified action words from verse 21, "submitting yourselves one to another" he was not telling wives or husbands "to submit!" in the non-Christian way. Instead, it was the Christian way of submitting between Christian wives and husbands that was an excellent model for all followers of Christ. Verse 24 echoed the ideas of verse 22.

In verse 23a, Paul used the word picture of a united joint-body. A husband and wife were members of one joint-body just as Christ and the church were members of one joint-body.

In the practical example in verse 25, Paul told husbands to love their wives with a godly love. Only Christian husbands could show this kind of love. As husbands practiced this godly love with their wives, so too godly love was practiced in interactions of the followers of Jesus with one another.

In the practical example in verses 28-29a, as husbands cared for their own physical bodies, so they were to love and care for their wives in Christian marriage. In the same way, there was to be love and care for one another in the body of Christ.

This set of examples had to do with life in the united joint-body of Christ and the church, as Paul stated in Ephesians 5:32. The same was true of the second set of examples.

In the second set of three practical examples from the Christian home, in Ephesians 5:33-6:9, Paul again showed the two actions that were part of submitting oneself one to another as followers of Christ. The two actions were: (1) to give of oneself and (2) to love the other.

The practical example in Ephesians 5:33, that was linked to submission one to another in verse 21, had to do with a Christian man and woman who were husband and wife. If this husband and wife had children, then the practical example in Ephesians 6:1-4 applied to them. If they also had servants, then the practical example in 6:5-9 also applied.

The great mystery transformed every relationship of the couple in their household. Each of these transformed relationships were examples of how to apply Ephesians 5:21 and submit one to the other in respect of Christ!

According to the first Christian husband and wife example in verse 31, they were to show "love" and "respect" as an example of the unity of believers with Christ. Some followers of Christ have not yet married. Some have lost their spouse in death or through divorce. Paul himself was single. Yet all believers shared in the wonderful unity of Christ and each other.

Taken out of context, Ephesians 5:33 has been misunderstood. Some translations have inserted the action word "to obey" for "to respect." But the action word "to obey" was only used for children (Ephesians 6:1) and for servants (Ephesians 6:5) and not for spouses.

In the practical example in Ephesians 6:1-4, if a husband and wife were parents, this practical example applied to them. Children had the responsibility to obey their parents (6:1-3).

By the time children were old enough to understand Paul's words to them from the Ten Commandments (Deuteronomy 5:16), many had already chosen to repent and were born-again members in the united spiritual relationship with Christ. For the period of their childhood, they were required to obey, and afterwards to honor, their father and their mother.

Jesus did this. As a child, he obeyed his parents while he lived inside the family circle with them (Luke 2:40). When Jesus was old enough, he became a full member of society after his examination by the religious leaders in Jerusalem. From that time on, as a young adult he honored his parents and submitted himself to them (Luke 2:51-52).

In verse 4, Paul turned from addressing Christian children to addressing their Christian parents. The Greek word for "parents" in Ephesians 6:4 was the same Greek word used in Hebrews 11:23. There, it designated the "parents" of Moses who hid him for three months. This word was like the word "brothers" which included brothers and sisters in Christ (Colossians 1:2).

Paul warned Christian parents against "embittering" or "provoking to wrath" their children. Parents were to be respectful in their dealings with their children. The action word used in verse 4, "to nourish" or bring them up, was the same one used in Ephesians 5:29. There it was an action taken by Christ, "nourish and cherish one's own flesh, as Christ does the church."

Both parents were responsible to nourish their children "in the discipline and admonition of the Lord." This important responsibility was taught throughout God's word, (Deuteronomy 6:6-7, Psalm 78:4, 2 Timothy 3:15).

According to the example in Ephesians 6:5-9, if a husband and wife had servants, this practical example applied to them. Most people living in the cities like Ephesus at the time of Paul were slaves or servants. Very many of them responded to the Good News and so the local gatherings of believers included many slaves and servants.

Paul's advice to servants and masters illustrated how, even in the context of the obedience required in the servant-master relationship, submitting one to another could be practiced in everyday life, especially in the context of Christian households.

Paul cautioned servants to do everything as if they were serving God and not just their masters (Ephesians 6:5-8). This was how Jacob's righteous son, Joseph, had lived when he was sold and taken to Egypt to be a slave. He knew God watched all he did. As he obeyed his masters, he pleased God.

Christian servants of earthly masters were first of all servants of Christ. The earthly work they did was to be done with good will, as service to the Lord! This pleased God who would reward them for their service.

The position of obedience was not necessarily a permanent one. Children grew up. Slaves could be set free. But honoring and serving were always actions pleasing to the Lord.

Masters in Christ, whether the husband or the wife, were not to threaten their servants (Ephesians 5:9). Paul referred to God's instructions for masters from Leviticus 25:43. Masters were to "respect" God. This, too, was a link back to Ephesians 5:21.

How could Paul tell masters to treat servants this way? Jesus turned his servants into his friends! Jesus told followers to treat each other the same way.

In John 15:15 and 17 Jesus said, "No longer do I call you servants, for a servant does not know what his master is doing; but I have called you friends, for all things that I heard from My Father I have made known to you. ... These things I command you, that you love one another" (NKJV).

***

The basic Christian church. Controlled by the Spirit, all followers of Christ sang to God and thanked God (5:19b-20). All were teachers and encouragers from the Word of God (Ephesians 5:19). All were learners from one another who applied what they learned (5:21). All gave of themselves for one another, and all loved and cared for one another (5:25b). Finally, all prayed for one another, as well (Ephesians 6:18).

The acts of the Spirit. There were seven acts of the Spirit in the lives of the followers of Christ. All followers of Christ needed to practice these acts in their daily lives.

Two acts of the Spirit were vertical — they dealt with a person's interaction with God. This was evidence of the new life that Christ gives to those who were born again.

Five acts of the Spirit were horizontal — they dealt with followers of Jesus interacting with one another. This was evidence of new life in the individuals who together made up the members of the body of Christ.

Singing and making music from your heart to the Lord. (Ephesians 5:19b)
Thanking always God the Father for everything. (Ephesians 5:20)

Speaking to one another (teaching and encouraging) from God's Word. (Ephesians 5:19, Colossians 3:16)
Submitting oneself to one another's teaching and encouragement from God's Word. (Ephesians 5:21)
Giving oneself sacrificially to one another, "as Christ" did. (Ephesians 5:23b, 25b)
Loving and caring for one another, "as Christ" did. (Ephesians 5:25, 29-30)
Praying one for another on all occasions with all kinds of prayers and requests. (Ephesians 6:18)

By practicing the seven acts of the Spirit — singing, thanking, speaking, submitting, giving, loving, praying — all followers of Christ grew in their relationship to God and built up one another in the body of Christ (Ephesians 4:12-13).

The helpers in the church. In addition, some of the followers were gifted by Christ to help build up the whole church (Ephesians 4:11-12). There were four kinds of helpers who did this — (1) messengers, (2) announcers, (3) harvesters and (4) nurturers.

It is helpful to picture the local church as follows (see the following illustration). The church is a circle of light.

In the church are the followers of Christ. They are the sheep in the flock of Christ. Some are mature in Christ, some are newborn in Christ, and some are in between. They practice the acts of the Spirit. They speak to and submit to one another. They use spiritual gifts distributed to each of them for the good of the body of Christ (1 Corinthians 12:7, Romans 12:4-8). Most of all they love one another (1 Corinthians 13).

Everything outside the circle of light is spiritual darkness. Those who live in this darkness are pictured as goats. They need to learn the good news of Christ. They need to be miraculously born again as newborn lambs and to be transferred from the darkness into the light.

Messengers take the light of the Word of God to those who live in darkness, outside the church. They tell the message of the light, the Good News of salvation. All those who are outside the church are the goats. Some are drawn to the light and listen. Some turn away.

Harvesters have one foot in the light and one foot in the darkness. They receive the goats which are drawn to the light and seek God. The harvesters tell the way of salvation to the goats and a wonderful miracle occurs to the goats who believe in Christ. They are born again as baby lambs! The harvesters bring in the newborn lambs to be cared for by the nurturers and all the other sheep.

Nurturers make sure the newborn lambs receive milk and care. They also watch over and teach the growing lambs and full-grown sheep.

Announcers are inside the church. They proclaim the Word of God to the sheep who are fed and strengthened by it.

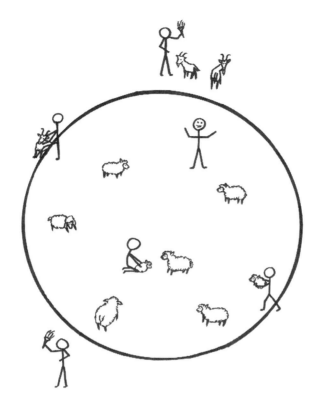

In the light of Eden. The union of the first husband and wife with each other and with God in Genesis 2 was followed in Genesis 3 by Satan's attack. In Ephesians 5:15-6:9, the union of Christ and the church was followed by Christians standing firm against Satan's attacks, in Ephesians 6:11-18.

The sixth passage of Ephesians 4-6, Ephesians 6:10-18, began with the words "therefore" "stand." Followers of Christ filled with the Spirit, together in Christ, could stand against the attacks of Satan!

Paul ended with a last action that followers of Christ did who were filled with the Spirit. They prayed! "And pray in the Spirit on all occasions with all kinds of prayers and requests. With this in mind, be alert and always keep on praying for all the Lord's people" (Ephesians 6:18).

In the Garden of Eden, there was creation and an attack.
1. Two walked in unity with one another and with God (Genesis 2:25)
2. They were attacked by Satan and were defeated (Genesis 3:1-6)

In the Church, there was a new creation and successful defense against attack.
1. Christ and the church were united (Ephesians 5:32)
2. Believers stood firm against Satan's attacks (Ephesians 6:10-18)

The unity of the church with Christ through salvation was better even than the unity experienced in the Garden of Eden. Together with Christ, empowered by his Spirit, believers could successfully stand against the attacks of Satan!

***

Share your thinking: Discussion questions on Chapter 2 of *Women & Men.*

With each answer, note the verse, or verses, where it was found.

1. How many passages in Ephesians 4-6 started with "therefore" and "walk" in Greek?

2. Where did the passage begin and end that talked about being controlled by the Spirit?

3. What was every believer to do, one to another, according to Ephesians 5:19 and 21?

4. What was the link in verse 22 to verse 21? What was verse 22 about?

5. What was the great mystery?

6. Do you practice the seven acts of the Spirit?

7. "Always let a Bible passage speak for itself." Did you discover the real meaning of a verse?

Chapter Three

Corrected and Restored to Service by Christ

Some teachers go astray

Paul made a brief visit to the important city of Ephesus on his second missionary journey. He taught in the synagogue and was well received. He left behind him at Ephesus Priscilla and Acquila, who were with him the many months he taught in Corinth (Acts 18:19-26).

When Paul returned to Ephesus, he stayed for several years. Paul taught in public and in the house churches. One group of believers was meeting in the home of Priscilla and Acquila (1 Corinthians 16:19).

In his letter to the Ephesians, Paul revealed that the Spirit of Christ chose certain ones among them to serve the rest (Ephesians 4:11). The responsibility of those who served the others was to equip the rest of God's people to do his work (Ephesians 4:12a).

After Paul visited Ephesus later in his ministry, he wrote a letter to Timothy (1 Timothy 1-6). Paul had discovered that some, who were gifted by the Holy Spirit to teach and equip the other believers in Ephesus, had become false teachers.

Their teaching and their behavior led other people astray and caused controversies to grow in Ephesus. When Paul left Ephesus, to continue his work elsewhere, he left Timothy there to correct the ones who could be corrected.

> ... stay there in Ephesus so that you may command certain ones not to teach false doctrines any longer nor to devote themselves to myths and endless genealogies. These promote controversies rather than God's work — which is by faith. ... Some have wandered away from these and turned to meaningless talk. They want to be teachers of the law, but they do not know what they are talking about or what they so confidently affirm. (1 Timothy 1:3b-7)

Paul started his letter with "Dear Timothy" (1 Timothy 1:2). Since both Paul and Timothy knew the believers at Ephesus, Paul did not need to write out every name or every detail about what was wrong.

Paul expected the others in Ephesus to learn the contents of his letter too and to cooperate with Timothy. At the end of the letter, Paul wrote, "Grace be with all of you" (1 Timothy 6:21).

First, Paul wrote about his own life. Then, he wrote about those who had strayed. He told Timothy how to deal with them.

Who taught at Ephesus? When Paul wrote his earlier letter to all the Ephesians, he taught that the "body of Christ" included Jesus himself, and all believers. They were members of one spiritual joint-body (Ephesians 3:4-6). In that body, every believer taught and counseled one another as part of life together in the Spirit (Ephesians 5:19, 21; Colossians 3:16).

The group of nurturers among the believers who served the rest by teaching God's Word, Paul had called "shepherd-teachers" in the Greek language (Ephesians 4:11). In 1 Timothy, Paul called them by another Greek word. He called them "overseers." They all were "able to teach" (3:1-2).

Some believers nurtured the rest as "overseers."
They taught God's Word.

Some of these overseers had gone astray. They were teaching false doctrines. They were teaching strange myths. And they taught in ways that were not right! Timothy's mission was to stop them, correct them and restore them.

Three sections. Paul organized his letter to Timothy in three major sections. The first section was the shortest. The last section was the longest.

The first section was about Paul, himself (1 Timothy 1:1-17). The second section was about three groups of people who had the responsibility to serve, inside and outside the body of Christ (1 Timothy 1:18-3:16). The third section was about Timothy (1 Timothy 4-6).

Section 1. About Paul (1 Timothy 1:1-17)
Section 2. About those with responsibilities (1 Timothy 1:18-3:15)
Section 3. About Timothy (1 Timothy 4-6)

Paul taught that Jesus Christ was the one who made others faithful in their service. In each section of his letter he used two Greek words for Jesus. The words were "faithful" (*pistos*) and "Word" (*logos*). Jesus, was the "faithful Word."

These two words were used near the end of the first section. They were used in the middle of the second section. They were was used near the start of the third section.

The "faithful Word" and Paul (1 Timothy 1:15)
The "faithful Word" and the corrected overseers (1 Timothy 3:1)
The "faithful Word" and Timothy (1 Timothy 4:9)

In 1 Timothy 1:1-17, Paul told how he had been a great sinner. But he was shown mercy because he acted in ignorance and unbelief (1 Timothy 1:13). God took this into account and Jesus, the "faithful Word," made him faithful to serve (1 Timothy 1:15)!

In 1 Timothy 1:18-3:16, Paul wrote about three groups of people. First, he gave advice about were those inside the church who had gone astray on purpose (1 Timothy 1:18-20). Second, he gave advice about those outside the church who had the power to persecute believers (1 Timothy 2:1-7). Finally, he gave advice about the teachers in the church who had gone astray (1 Timothy 2:8-15). Jesus, the "faithful Word," could restore them (1 Timothy 3:1)!

In 1 Timothy 4:1-6:21, Paul focused on Timothy. He had believed in Christ and was faithful from his youth. This, too, was because of the work of Jesus. He was made fit for service by the "faithful Word" (1 Timothy 4:9).

The "faithful Word." In 1 Timothy, when Paul wrote that Jesus was the "faithful Word," others knew what he meant. John called Jesus the "Word." He began his Gospel of John, not with the birth of Jesus, but with the work of the "Word" "in the beginning."

In the beginning was the Word, and the Word was with God, and the Word was God. He was with God in the beginning. Through him all things were made; without him nothing was made that has been made. ... The Word became flesh and made his dwelling among us. ... We have seen his glory, the glory of the One and Only, who came from the Father, full of grace and truth (from John 1:1-14, NIV).

The Greek word "*logos*" — or "word" — had another meaning, too. It could mean a "saying." In 1 Timothy 1:15, after calling Jesus the "faithful Word," Paul attached a "saying." The saying was that "Christ Jesus came into the world to save sinners."

This one time, Paul used the word "*logos*" to mean two things at the same time, both "Word" and "saying." Each meaning reinforced the same idea. Jesus was faithful to save.

The word play on "logos" did not need to be made every time. The main meaning that Jesus was the faithful Word made sense by itself. The saying could be kept in mind, without repeating it.

Paul used the double meaning of "saying" only the first time in 1 Timothy. The second and third times he used the two words, he did not add a well-known "saying." His focus was on Jesus, the "faithful Word."

***

Paul's three sins (1 Timothy 1:12-17). Early in his letter, Paul wrote a list of many sins (1 Timothy 1:9b-10):

... lawbreakers and rebels, the ungodly and sinful, the unholy and irreligious; those who kill their fathers or mothers, murderers, adulterers and perverts, slave traders and liars and perjurers — and whatever else is contrary to the sound doctrine that conforms to the glorious gospel of the blessed God, which he entrusted to me (NIV).

Then, Paul listed his own three sins (1 Timothy 1:13). First, Paul was a blasphemer because he had spoken evil of

Jesus. Second, he had persecuted believers in Christ. Third, he had disrupted their gatherings.

Paul was (1) a blasphemer, (2) a persecutor, and (3) a disrupter.

In his early years, Paul, who was then called Saul, was a student who had come to Jerusalem to study under the respected Jewish teacher, Gamaliel. Paul followed all the strict rules the Jews had made for Pharisees to follow. But this did not make him loving and good. Instead, he became critical and cruel.

The Good News came to Paul's synagogue, the Synagogue of the Freedmen (Acts 6:8-10). Stephen, a believer and a servant of the other believers in Jesus, announced that Jesus was God and had died for the sins of the world. Some rejected the wisdom of Stephen and the Holy Spirit and argued with him.

Since his accusers could not stand up to his words, his critics decided to blame Stephen falsely for blasphemy, a crime punishable by death (Acts 6:11, Numbers 15:29-31). They seized Stephen and accused him before the high court of the Jews where he was condemned. Then, he was dragged outside the city and put to death while Jesus watched from heaven! Paul was there. He approved of Stephen's execution (Acts 6:11-8:1). Paul did not believe that Jesus was God.

The day of Stephen's death, a great persecution broke out against the believers in Jerusalem. Paul persecuted the believers and disrupted their meetings. He "made havoc of the church, entering every house, and dragging off men and women, committing them to prison" (Acts 8:3, NKJV).

Afterward, Paul was still "breathing threats and murder against the disciples." He asked for official letters from the High Priest to go to synagogues outside the borders of Israel. He got them and was an official persecutor of believers (Acts 9:1-2). He planned to enter the synagogues and arrest any who believed in Jesus and bring them back to Jerusalem as prisoners.

As Paul and his companions walked to the city of Damascus, he was brought up short by a blindingly bright person who spoke to him. It was Jesus! He told Paul that his persecution of his followers was persecution of himself (Acts 9:3-6).

Paul had set out from Jerusalem intending to sanitize the synagogues by getting rid of the followers of a fake. He had not meant to rebel against God! He had sinned "in ignorance and unbelief" (1 Timothy 1:13b).

Paul had not rebelled against God on purpose.

Paul arrived in Damascus, physically blind, and convinced that he had been spiritually blind. Jesus had mercy on Paul and "judged him faithful by appointing Paul to his service" (1 Timothy 1:12, RSV).

Had Paul asked to go outside of Israel to the distant synagogues? Jesus confirmed that this would be his territory of service. But, Jesus changed Paul's mission. Instead of persecuting Jesus and the followers of Jesus, he would bear the name of Jesus wherever he went and suffer persecution for it (Acts 9:15-18).

After a few days with the believers, Paul announced in the synagogues of Damascus that Jesus was the Promised One, Savior of the world (Acts 9:20-22). To the amazement of all, Paul became the messenger of Christ the Savior to the Jews and especially those who were not Jews.

By the time he wrote to Timothy, Paul knew from much experience that Jesus, the Word, was always faithful! He closed the first section of his letter with a word of praise to God (1 Timothy 1:17).

***

Three groups in Ephesus (1 Timothy 1:18-3:16). Paul often gave a list near the start of his letters. The list pointed to what was coming next in his letter.

In 1 Timothy, the list is found in his three sins — Paul had been (1) a blasphemer, (2) a persecutor, and (3) a disrupter (1 Timothy 1:13). In section two of his letter, Paul wrote about groups of people in Ephesus who corresponded to each one of his three sins.

Paul commented about those who were guilty of his first sin in a few words. He commented about those who had the power to commit his second sin with more words. He commented to Timothy about the group guilty of his third sin with the most words.

Blasphemers at Ephesus (1 Timothy 1:18-20)
Persecutors at Ephesus (1 Timothy 2:1-7)
Disrupters at Ephesus (1 Timothy 2:8-3:16)

Blasphemers (1 Timothy 1:18-20). After repeating his greeting to Timothy and the reason for his letter (1 Timothy 1:18), Paul drew a contrast between Timothy, who had not gone astray, and several Ephesians who had gone astray. They were blasphemers.

Paul named two of them — Hymenaeus and Alexander. This group received severe correction because they were first-degree blasphemers who had willfully sinned. They had rejected faith and a good conscience and made a shipwreck of their faith.

Paul turned them over to Satan to be taught not to blaspheme (1 Timothy 1:19-20). There was a big difference in the treatment of Paul who was a second-degree blasphemer, and Hymenaeus and Alexander who were first-degree blasphemers.

There was a big difference in the treatment of first-degree sinners and second-degree sinners.

Persecutors (1 Timothy 2:1-7). Next, Paul wrote to Timothy about those who had political authority — "for kings and all those in authority" (2:2). They had the power to persecute the Christians in Ephesus. Before he believed in Christ, Paul had been one of these — a persecutor with authority from the high priest in Jerusalem.

In Ephesus, there had already been a noisy demonstration against Christians led by those who made idols (Acts 19:23-40). This disturbance had been put down. Paul urged believers to pray for kings and all others in authority to leave them in peace and not persecute them (1 Timothy 2:1-2).

Paul also wanted those who had the authority to persecute believers to come to know Christ just like he had. This was God's will even for them (1 Timothy 2:3-7). Paul knew from personal experience that they could come to Christ. They could believe like Paul had believed!

Disrupters (1 Timothy 2:8-3:16). Those whose sin corresponded to Paul's third sin were the disrupters. Correcting these "shepherd-teachers" (Ephesians 4:11), or "overseers" (1 Timothy 3:1), who had been false teachers was the work of Timothy. In the beginning of 1 Timothy, Paul had written,

> As I urged you when I went into Macedonia, stay there in Ephesus so that you may command *some* **not to teach false doctrines any longer or to devote themselves to myths and endless genealogies**. Such things promote controversial speculations rather than advancing God's work .... (1 Timothy 1:3-4).

The "some" in the church in Ephesus were a group of some of the men and some of the women teaching overseers who had been teaching false doctrines to the rest. Not all of the teaching overseers had been false teachers. Perhaps not most, nor even half of the overseers had been teaching incorrectly. But a subgroup of the men and women overseers had been doing so.

When he left Ephesus, Paul had told Timothy to command them not to teach false doctrines and myths any longer. By the time Timothy received the letter from Paul, it is very likely he had carried out this command and had stopped these teaching overseers from teaching incorrectly.

After Paul left, Timothy had time to stop the false teachers.
Then, Paul wrote Timothy how to correct and restore them to service.

In 1 Timothy 2:8-3:16, Paul told Timothy how to correct the false teachers and restore them to service. He first addressed the subgroup of the men overseers who had engaged in false teaching and incorrect practices. Then he addressed the subgroup of the women overseers who had engaged in false teaching and incorrect practices. Paul had called them "some" or "certain ones." This word applied to both the men and the women.

The Greek word Paul used in his list for his own third sin was too harsh to apply to any believer, even to false teachers among the overseers. It described what Paul did before becoming a believer in Christ (1 Timothy 1:13). He did not use it for the false teachers, but he described their disruptive acts (1 Timothy 2:8 regarding the men; 2:9b, 12 regarding the women).

Paul's words about dealing with the disruptive false teachers were grouped into three parts. The first part, and the shortest, was for the group of wayward men (1 Timothy 2:8). The second part, which was longer, was for the group of wayward women (1 Timothy 2:9-15). The third part, which was the longest of all, was about their restoration by the "faithful Word."

Paul wrote about the character of faithful teachers (1 Timothy 3:1-13). Paul ended his words in 1 Timothy 1:18-3:16 by restating his reasons for writing and with a summary of good teaching (1 Timothy 3:14-16).

> **Some men.** "I want" correct teaching from the men (1 Timothy 2:8)
> **Some women.** "Likewise" from the women (1 Timothy 2:9-15)
> **Both groups.** The "faithful Word" and faithful servants (1 Timothy 3:1-16)

Links. In 1 Timothy 2:8, Paul wrote about the group of men Timothy was correcting. In 1 Timothy 2:9-15, Paul wrote about the group of women he was correcting.

In verse 9, Paul linked these two groups together. He did it by using the word "Likewise" without adding any action words for the women.

This meant that the action in verse 8 was to be brought down and used for verse 9. The wayward group of men of verse 8 and the wayward group of women of verses 9-15 were linked together by a shared action.

In 1 Timothy 3:1, as in 1 Timothy 1:3, Paul referred to "some," who aspired to oversight. This "some" in 1 Timothy 3:1 did not mean "everyone." It referred to those men and women Timothy was correcting (in 1 Timothy 2:8-15) as one group.

1. Some men (1 Timothy 2:8). Paul wrote what he wanted from them. Paul also wrote what he did not want from them.

Do what? Paul used the one action word — "to-pray" — to stand in the place of two action words. He used this same action word for the men and for the women. In Greek, it was possible to use just one action word to stand for two action words that commonly went together.

In his letter to the church at Corinth (1 Corinthians 11:4-5), there was a reference to men and women who prayed *and* prophesied in church. In 1 Timothy, they prayed *and* taught in church.

This is what Paul wanted Timothy to correct in Ephesus. Timothy was to teach the overseers who had gone astray as they led worship in their prayer and in their teaching.

Where? In Jerusalem after Pentecost, the believers in Jesus gathered together with one another. In Christ, they belonged together as much as the parts of a body belong together.

The twelve original messengers of Jesus, such as Peter, John and Matthew, were there among them. The believers devoted themselves to the messengers' teaching ... and to prayer (Acts 2:42, 5:12, 42).

Years later in far off Ephesus, in the absence of the original messengers who had walked beside Jesus, the Holy Spirit gifted some of the believers to serve the rest to build up the body of Christ (Ephesians 4:11).

Paul's advice was about those who were teaching the believers when they gathered in every house church in Ephesus. One way to say this was *"in every place."*

This three-word Greek phrase in 1 Timothy 2:8, "in every place" did not mean "everywhere" nor "all over the world." To the Jews, "place" meant "meeting-place," or "place of prayer." The Christian believers used that word for their meeting places, too (1 Corinthians 1:2, 1 Thessalonians 1:8).

Stop what? Paul told this group of men to lift up "holy hands." Did they have unholy hands? In what way? Paul gave no more details about their sin, but Timothy understood. Some behavior caused their hands to be unholy. They were to act correctly so that they could lift up holy hands.

The way they lived and the false doctrines they taught stirred up "wrath and dissension." If they had not sinned and had taught what was false, they would not have caused these reactions among the rest of the believers. Their sin and their false teaching needed to be replaced by what was good!

Here is a paraphrase of 1 Timothy 2:8, based on the Greek of this verse:

I want these men to pray and teach correctly in church, lifting up holy hands, no longer sinning and disrupting the church with their behavior and false teaching which had caused wrath and dissension.

2. Some women (1 Timothy 2:9-15). Here is a paraphrase of the beginning of Paul's words about women teachers. It shows the link Paul made in Greek to his words about the men:

Likewise — I want these women to pray and teach correctly in church — adorning themselves in orderly clothing, with propriety and moderation, not with hair braided with gold or pearls, or with costly clothing, but as women who correctly teach the Good News and do good works.

Paul wrote what he wanted them to do. He wrote what he did not want them to do. Paul's words about these women were longer than his words about the men. He used several word patterns to organize his words.

Word patterns. Paul gave only one command to Timothy in all these verses from 9-15. It was, "**Let learn!**" This was the main idea of verse 11.

This command in verse 11 stood in the middle of a seven-point word pattern in verses 9-15. Everything else was subordinate to what Timothy was to do — see that these women were taught so that they might learn more fully.

1. Three ways to act correctly (1 Timothy 2:9a).
2. Two ways not to act (1 Timothy 2:9b).
3. How to teach and act correctly (1 Timothy 2:10).
4. **"Let these women learn!" (1 Timothy 2:11).**
5. How not to teach (1 Timothy 2:12).
6. Why treat them this way (1 Timothy 2:13-15a).
7. The corrected teachers act faithfully (1 Timothy 2:15b).

In 1 Timothy 2:9-10, Paul listed three ways to act correctly. Then, he listed two incorrect ways to act. Then, he listed two more correct ways to act.

Correct: (1) wear orderly clothing, with (2) propriety and (3) moderation (2:9a)
Incorrect: (1) not with hair braided with gold or pearls, or costly clothing (2:9b)
Correct: (1) dress as teachers of godliness, (2) do good works (2:10)

In cities like Ephesus in Paul's day, there were many slaves and servants, both male and female. More than eight out of ten people were servants or slaves. The majority of believers were poor servants or slaves. But there were some believers who were wealthy.

Correct. Paul wanted women teachers to do things that any believer, poor or rich, could do. He wanted them to adorn themselves with orderly clothing, propriety and moderation (1 Timothy 2:9a).

Incorrect. Some of the women teachers in Ephesus had been immodest in the way they dressed. It was incorrect behavior to arrange hair with very expensive ornaments, such as gold and pearls, and to wear costly clothing (1 Timothy 2:9b, see also 1 Timothy 6:17-21).

Correct. Paul wanted women teachers, poor or rich, to teach "godliness" — what Jesus and his messengers taught — and do good works (1 Timothy 2:10). Paul himself taught about godliness (1 Timothy 3:16). Professing, or teaching, godliness was the correct way for women teachers to act.

Paul's command. In 1 Timothy 2:11-12, Paul told Timothy to retrain the women teachers who had dressed improperly and disrupted the church by their false teaching. These two points were made in one sentence, with two parts. The main idea was in verse 11. In verse 12, Paul added details but did not change the main idea in verse 11.

Some people wanted to learn. Timothy was to let them learn! He was to make sure they were fully instructed.

The Greek words in Paul's command in verse 11 had four parts:

(1) woman / (2) in quietness / (3) let learn! / (4) paying attention

Woman. Who did Paul have in mind? Paul began his command to Timothy with the Greek word — "woman" — all by itself, without an article in front of it.

He didn't write "the" woman. He didn't write "all" women or "some" women. He wrote — "woman." Using a Greek word this way in this context stood for a "sub-group" of women.

Paul's advice was not about all women believers in Christ, nor even all women teachers in church. Paul had in mind a "sub-group" of the women overseers.

These were the women who had become false teachers. Among the all the women teachers, Timothy was to correct only the ones who had taught incorrectly, or "these women."

1 Timothy 2:11 is a verse about a sub-group of the women teachers.

In quietness. Paul wrote the words — "in quietness" — two times. These words were important for their meaning and they were important for how they were used in the sentence.

First he wrote the words "in quietness" right after the first word — "woman" — at the start of verse 11. Second, he wrote them at the very end of verse 12. In the Greek language, repeating these words in this word pattern was called an "inclusio." It was used to show that everything in between the repeated words was grouped together as one idea.

What did a person do "in quietness"? A person learned "in quietness." Paul was "in quietness" when he was taught by his own Jewish teacher, Gamaliel.

Let learn! Immediately after the words "in quietness," Paul wrote, "Let learn!" This was the only action word that was a command to Timothy in these verses. This action word was the most important thing Timothy was to do.

Some Bible translations make it look like there was another command in verse 12. But, there was not another command. "Let learn" was the only one.

In short, Paul's one command to Timothy in verses 11-12 was:

"This sub-group of women teachers, in quietness, let learn! ... in quietness."

This was not the way Paul had treated the rebellious group of blasphemers. They would "learn" from Satan. The Greek word for "learn" that Paul used for them meant "education through punishment" (1 Timothy 1:20)!

This was not the action word Paul used in verse 11. The action word in verse 11 had nothing to do with punishment.

It was, "*Let learn!*" This action word was used for anyone who *learned* from their teacher.

Paul didn't need to write *gather* these women together and *make* them learn. They already wanted to learn. Timothy was to *let* them learn. He was to do this even if some people did not want to let them learn.

When Timothy had stopped all the Christian false teachers in Ephesus, these women realized they needed to learn what they should have been teaching. This is what they wanted to learn. What was the right way to behave when teaching? What should they teach to the rest of the believers?

Paying attention. Paul's last words in verse 11, "in all subjection," have been misunderstood. In the context of learning these words meant "paying attention." Paying attention to a teacher was a part of learning. This action went along with "in silence." Both were proper ways to learn.

Who were they paying attention to? Students pay attention to their teachers. Most likely Timothy was their teacher.

There may have been other teachers for them, too. They may have come from the women or men teachers who had not gone astray. Priscilla and Acquila were in Ephesus. They had already corrected Apollos (Acts 18:24-26). They could retrain this sub-group of women teachers.

There was a reason Paul wanted this sub-group of women teachers to learn. The Jews described a teacher-in-training as someone who "learns in order to teach and that learns in order to practice" (m. 'Abot 6:6). Paul had mentioned this double purpose, *(1) to teach* and *(2) to practice*, in 1 Timothy 2:10 where he wrote about women overseers (1) teaching godliness and (2) doing good works.

Verse 12 was connected to verse 11. It was in the same sentence. The words in these two verses were grouped together. The words "paying attention" were used early in verse 11 and at the end of verse 12.

The main idea of Paul's command was found in verse 11. Additional details were added in verse 12. Some people have treated the action words in verse 12 with the same importance as Paul's command in verse 11. This is not correct!

Paul's words in verse 12, in Greek, were made up of two parts:

(1) I am not permitting them / (2) to teach men incorrectly

"Them." Who did Paul have in mind? He meant the sub-group of women overseers who had been teaching incorrectly.

Verse 12 continued his words from verse 11. Paul was not permitting false teaching where he was, just like he had left Timothy in Ephesus to stop false teaching there.

In verses 11 and 12 Paul wrote one basic message:

There is no place for improper teaching. It must be stopped. Then the false teachers must be corrected. Let them learn.

For Paul, the main idea of verse 11 applied where he was in Achaia. Some women teachers there had gone astray in a similar way. And they were learning as they were retrained for service.

"To teach incorrectly." In part two of verse 12, Paul gave more details about their false teaching. In 1 Timothy 2:9b, Paul had described the incorrect way they were *dressing*. In verse 12, Paul described the incorrect way they were *teaching*. They were doing something wrong.

What was it? The action was "to teach a man in an incorrect way."

Paul used two action words and put them together into one action. The two action words were *didaskein* and *authentein*. He used two joining words in Greek to put them together.

It was an *authentein*-way of teaching (1 Timothy 2:12) that involved men. It was an incorrect way that resulted in disruption of the church.

What was this incorrect way to teach? Paul and Timothy knew the details. So did the believers in both places where Paul and Timothy were, but Paul did not write out the details.

Because the meaning of the word *authentein* is not well-understood in modern days, it is difficult to say more. But, this was not the main point. The command in verse 11 was the main idea. Timothy was to let them learn! Any incorrect teaching that disrupted the church was not allowed.

The false teachers were silenced. Then, they learned and were retrained.

These verses, 11-12, were not about wives and husbands. They were about a sub-group of the women teachers.

In 1 Timothy 2:13-15a, Paul recommended gentle treatment for the women who had become false teachers. Perhaps others in Ephesus wanted harsher treatment for them.

Paul gave the reason for his instructions. Paul saw these women in the light of Eden.

Paul saw these women in the light of Eden!

In his words, Paul did not follow the order in which things happened in the Garden of Eden. He reorganized things in a pattern that showed the two persons in the Garden as individuals.

First, Paul called the woman "Eve" (1 Timothy 2:13). But, at the moment in time he referred to her she was not called "Eve" (Genesis 2:22-23)! That happened later (Genesis 3:20). By using the two names "Eve" and "Adam," Paul treated them as two separate persons.

Second, they were sinners in different ways (1 Timothy 2:14). At the tree in the Garden, the woman took her bite first. Then the man took his bite. But Paul wrote about Adam first! This also made a distinction between the two persons.

Third, Paul pointed out the man was not deceived when he ate. He decided to rebel against God. Then, Paul pointed to the woman. She ate the fruit after she was deceived by the "father of lies." She sinned, but she did not rebel against God as the man did!

Why did Paul point this out? Paul wanted Timothy to deal with the women false teachers in Ephesus like God dealt with the woman in Eden. God had treated Paul the same gentle way.

In the Garden of Eden, God made a distinction between the two sinners (Genesis 3:16-19). God, in the Garden, treated the woman gently, as a second-degree sinner.

Who in Ephesus was like Eve? The subgroup of women false teachers was like Eve.

Paul finished his words about Eve by reminding Timothy that she was saved through her faith in "the birth of the Child" whom God had promised to her (1 Timothy 15a). Belief in Christ was enough for Paul and these women, too.

Here is a paraphrase of Paul's words: "These women are not like Adam who decided to rebel against God. They are like Eve who was deceived and sinned. She (Eve) was saved through faith in the promised One."

Some have suggested that Paul wrote not about "the birth of the Child" but just about "childbirth" in general. In the light of Eden, the promise to the first woman was about conception of the Seed. It was not the physical childbirth.

Translations that insert the word childbirth into Genesis 3:16a are tempted to use the same word here. Many readers of such translations have been led to question the salvation of a woman according to her experiences in childbirth. How awful! How unnecessary!

The Greek words used in 1 Timothy 2:15 were "she" in the first part of the verse, and "they" in the second part of the verse. Paul finished his illustration from the life of Eve in the first part of the verse.

Next, Paul wrote about "they" in 1 Timothy 2:15b. Paul pointed back to the actions of the teachers who had not gone astray. "They" were the example of women teachers who taught correctly (1 Timothy 2:9a, 10).

In verse 15b, Paul summarized the good ways they acted. He wanted the corrected ones to persevere in faith, love, holiness and self-control (1 Timothy 15b).

3. Both groups (1 Timothy 3:1-13). Next, Paul wrote about Jesus, the "faithful Word." Reminding them about Jesus was his way to encourage the ones Timothy retrained. He wrote that Jesus could make faithful servants of "anyone who aspired to oversight" (1 Timothy 3:1).

Who was "anyone?" The answer was found by looking back to the people Paul was writing about. This word, "anyone," included the women overseers who had been teaching incorrectly (1 Timothy 2:9-15), and "anyone" included the men who had disrupted the church through their false teaching (1 Timothy 2:8).

"Anyone" included the women and men overseers Timothy corrected after they went astray.

Paul had been appointed for service that he might be an example for others (1 Timothy 1:16). Paul had been corrected and made fit for service by Jesus, "the faithful Word." Jesus, the "faithful Word," made the retrained women and men overseers fit to serve again. They were to be faithful and trustworthy teachers. Paul explained to Timothy how to judge their readiness to resume public ministry.

***

Faithful overseers (1 Timothy 3:1-7). They had to be faithful, too, in the way they lived. Not everyone would live exactly as Paul and Timothy did (unmarried, no fixed home), but they should live blamelessly as examples in every way that applied to them.

In all the Greek words in the first seven verses of 1 Timothy 3, not once did Paul use a word that applied only to men or only to women. Every word in verses 1-7 applied to all without distinction, women and men. This was also true of 1 Timothy 3:8-10.

Every word in verses 1-7 applied to all without distinction, women and men.

Some translations of the Bible seem to say these verses were only about men. However, all that led up to these verses was about men *and* women. Both the words meanings and the word patterns clearly include both women *and* men. Some translations need to be corrected so everyone can understand these verses more clearly.

Paul listed fifteen characteristics of faithful overseers. If a characteristic applied to a woman or a man, they had to pass this test before serving again.

Here are the characteristics: (1) blameless — the overall characteristic, (2) a faithful spouse, (3) able to exercise self-control, (4) sensible, (5) orderly, (6) hospitable, (7) able to teach, (8) not one who drinks too much, (9) not violent, (10) gentle, (11) not quarrelsome, (12) not a lover of money, (13) able to manage the household and have children that obey, (14) not a new believer, and (15) having a good reputation with those outside the church (1 Timothy 3:1b-7).

The first characteristic of a good overseer was the all important one. The others were to be followed as they applied to a person.

"Blameless" (1 Timothy 3:2). Overseers were to be blameless models of good living in Christ. This qualification was so important that Paul introduced it in Greek with, "It is necessary...."

Paul lived this way. As a result, he could invite others, like the believers who gathered together at the city of Philippi, to follow his example: "Join with others in following my example, brothers and sisters, and take note of those who live according to the pattern we gave you" (Philippians 3:17).

"A faithful spouse" (1 Timothy 3:2). This next characteristic, a faithful spouse (in Greek, a "one-wife-husband," *mias gynaikos andra*), applied to overseers who were married, whether or not they had children. This was the only place in the New Testament where these three Greek words were used exactly in this way.

In other places, where Paul had husbands only in mind, he said so. He used Greek words in a way that applied to men only — "husband of one wife" (1 Timothy 3:12, Titus 1:6).

In the mid-twentieth century, inscriptions of this unique three-word Greek saying were found by the French archaeologist and Bible translator, Lucien Deiss. He found these three words on some funeral inscriptions from the time of Paul in the area around Ephesus. They were found on the graves of men and women. Also, the words were written on the graves of both Jews and non-Jews.

When I interviewed him, Deiss said that "one-wife-husband" was a commonly-known "saying" that meant the person had lived as "a faithful spouse" as a wife or a husband. Overseers needed to be like this if they were married — a one-spouse kind of person in a faithful marriage relationship.

But, for a long time, these words have not been understood as a "saying." Translators and teachers have used other ideas about these three words, but they don't fit the situation or Paul's line of thought.

For example, this saying didn't require that an overseer had to be a man. It did not require an overseer to be married. For example, Paul did not have a wife (1 Corinthians 7:1-8).

And, for example, this saying was not about polygamy. Other passages in the Bible gave lessons against polygamy (Genesis 4:23-24). In fact, a survey of every case of polygamy in the Old Testament shows polygamy was a bad situation.

"Able to manage his or her own household well" (1 Timothy 3:4-5). If an overseer had children, it was important to be a good manager of the home. Paul wrote that an overseer had to manage "*his* or *her* own household well." Those who did so could be trusted to serve the believers in the local gatherings of the body of Christ.

Who could forget the lessons they learned in Ephesians 5:22-6:9 in the letter Paul had written to them? As spouses, they were in a wonderful one-flesh, united relationship. As Christians together, they were in an even better one-flesh, united relationship with each other and with Christ (Ephesians 5:31-32).

***

Faithful servants (deacons) (1 Timothy 3:8-13). In Philippians 1:1, Paul referred to two groups of people who served the rest of the believers: (1) the "overseers," and (2) the "servants" or deacons. Paul had these same groups in view in 1 Timothy 3:2-13.

The main difference between overseers and deacons was being "able to teach" (1 Timothy 3:2). Teaching was not on the list for deacons. Timothy's assignment in Ephesus was to correct false teachers, so a word about deacons was not strictly necessary. However, some deacons taught, like Stephen (Acts 8).

Paul began his advice about deacons with the words, "In the same way," or "Likewise." This referred to the men and women of 1 Timothy 3:1-7 who were made fit for service by the "faithful Word." Just as the ones who aspired to oversight could be made faithful, in the same way, the "faithful Word" could make fit men and women servants, or deacons.

In 1 Timothy 3:8-10, Paul listed seven characteristics for faithful deacons. They were to be: (1) worthy of respect, (2) not double-tongued, (3) not full of desire for wine (4) not pursuing dishonest gain, (5) faithful to the mystery of the faith with (6) a clear conscience, (7) blameless.

Paul gave advice for women deacons in verse 11 and advice for men deacons in verse 12. As for the **women** who were deacons, Paul told them to be worthy of respect, not slanderers, self-controlled, and faithful in all things (1 Timothy 3:11). As for the **men** who were deacons, he told them to work at being faithful husbands and to be responsible at home (1 Timothy 3:12).

It was good to serve faithfully! Paul wrote, "Those who have served well gain respect from others and great confidence in their faith in Christ Jesus" (1 Timothy 3:13).

In 1 Timothy 2:8-3:13, Paul organized his words in this way:

Men (1 Timothy 2:8)
Women (1 Timothy 2:9-15)
Both **Women** and *Men* (1 Timothy 3:1-7, 8-10)
Women (1 Timothy 3:11)
Men (1 Timothy 3:12)

In review. In 1 Timothy 2:8-15, Paul gave Timothy advice on how to correct false teachers. His recommendations took into account (1) not only the sin committed, but also (2) the heart motivation of the offender. In 1 Timothy 3:1-7, the women and men overseers who had been corrected were encouraged to aspire to, and to resume, ministry in the church, thanks to the "faithful Word!"

Some people have missed the importance of the way Paul divided the whole letter to Timothy into three sections by using the phrase the "faithful Word." They have also misunderstood the word pattern Paul used based on his three sins inside the second section of the letter in 1 Timothy 2:8-3:15. As a result, they have taken Paul's words out of context. When anyone bases their ideas on human imagination, and not God's revelation, it is easy to go astray.

Paul did not teach a lesson on "authority-of-a-husband" in 1 Timothy 2, or "leadership-by-men" in the church in 1 Timothy 3. He did not teach that "only married men could serve."

Instead, he encouraged the women and men, who were gifted by Christ to serve the rest of the believers, to do their work well. For those who went astray through ignorance or deception, they could look forward to serving again thanks to Jesus, the faithful Word!

The women and men who were gifted by Christ to serve were to be faithful servants of the rest.

Timothy. Paul addressed the third section of his letter (1 Timothy 4:1-6:21) to Timothy himself. Timothy's situation was different in several ways from that of Paul and that of the disrupters. Timothy had not lived a life of sin nor had he gone astray.

Paul warned Timothy that more people would fall away (1 Timothy 4:1-3). Timothy would need to be well-disciplined in his ministry (1 Timothy 4:6-8). But, "the faithful Word" (1 Timothy 4:9), would keep him strong in his effort to serve faithfully.

Timothy was to stay away from favoritism (1 Timothy 5:21) and was to test individuals before setting them apart for service (1 Timothy 5:22 and 3:10). Again, Paul told Timothy to keep a watch over himself and be on guard against opposition and any wandering away from the faith (1 Timothy 6:20-21).

The Book of Revelation, written by John after Paul's death, reported that Timothy's mission was successful! Jesus said to the believers at Ephesus, "I know ... you cannot bear those who are evil. You have tested those who say they are messengers and are not, and have found them liars ...." (Revelation 2:2). In the middle of a very corrupt and pagan society, the work of the "faithful Word" had been fruitful!

***

Share your thinking: Discussion questions on Chapter 3 of *Women & Men.*

With each answer, note the verse, or verses, where it was found.

1. What was the key phrase of two Greek words that Paul used in each Section of 1 Timothy?

2. Why did Paul leave Timothy at Ephesus?

3. How did Eve and Paul sin in the same way?

4. What was the command Paul gave Timothy in 2:11-12?

5. When you have gone astray, has Jesus been faithful to restore you? When?